Mr Brexit

Mr Brexit

My Plan for Britain's Glittering Economic Future

Sir Reginald Futtock

IndieBooks

Mr Brexit: My Plan for Britain's Glittering
Economic Future

By Sir Reginald Futtock

ISBN: 978-1-908041-44-9

Published by IndieBooks Ltd
Unit 9, 5-7 Wells Terrace, London N4 3JU

Set in Corbel 13/14

Printed by Biddles, King's Lynn, UK

1 3 5 7 9 8 6 4 2

Also by Sir Reginald Futtock

The Rough Guide to Offshore Tax Havens
Teach Yourself Creative Accounting
The Seven Secrets of Successful Sackings
The Art of the Steal

Forthcoming

Futtock's Fortunes

Contents

Acknowledgements   9

Introduction   11

The Great Divorce   17
*The European Menace – How We Were
Seduced – The Honeymoon Years –
Breaking Up – Moving Out*

Britain's Economic Scorecard   49
*The Single Market – Manufacturing – The
Service Sector – Technology – The Creative
Industries – Property – Agriculture*

Our Great New British Economic Miracle   95
*The New Economy – Wealth Creation –
Employment – Immigration – Competition –
International Trade – Exports*

Forging a New Britain   145
*Sovereignty Plus – A Leaner, Hungrier
Britain – Education – Health – The
Environment – National Assets – The
Challenge – The Negotiations – The Plan*

Acknowledgements

There are so many people that I could thank for helping me write this book. But in keeping with the post-Brexit mood of naked self-interest, I'm only going to mention those who may be helpful to me in the future.

So a huge thanks to my current wife Babs, for putting up with me and, just as importantly, putting up with Elenka, my current mistress. My heartfelt thanks also to Elenka, for putting up with Nastasia, also my current mistress; and to Nastasia, for putting up with Bonzo, my Bernese Mountainadoodle.

To my fellow industrialists, speculators, gropers, traitors, murderers and other members of the Clermont Club, living and dead, whose patriotic view of Britain's future potential has always been as inspiring as it is insane.

My fondest thanks to Poppaea, Magdalena and Funty, for help with the arduous research; to Frisby, my butler, whose caviar butties, accompanied by a decent bottle of Montrachet, kept me going through many a long morning's writing; and to 'KCK', my special adviser K. Calvin Kilman III, for coming over from Washington and daring to think the unelectable.

And a final thank you to all those who voted to leave the European Union. Your loss is very definitely my gain.

Mr Brexit

Introduction

A Calling can come upon a man anywhere. For me, the Call came in a religious bric-a-brac shop on the Island of St Honore, just off the Cote d'Azur, as a bulky monk called Brother Mary kneed me in the balls, while Elenka yelped him on with assorted screams of 'Rapist! Evictor! Monster! Bankrupt!'

As my head bounced off a display case of Lives of The Saints, I was reminded of dear old Peter Rachmann and of St Francis of Assisi; who notoriously lost his grip after hearing The Lord say: 'Francis, go and repair my House, which is being destroyed'.

Once I had pacified Elenka, and explained to Brother Mary that my failure to pay for the snow-globe of Pope Paul XXIII was pure oversight, I was able to retrieve my phone from beneath the confessional box. It was the No 10 switchboard.

'Is that Sir Reginald? I have the Prime Minister for you.'

Much as one looks down on Ms May – would she, one wonders, have made it into the cabinet under Maggie? – a PM is still a PM. I sat up a little straighter as in those rather chilly tones – reminiscent of a no-nonsense school matron – she came to the point.

'We need a Plan for life after Brexit. I can't come up with one. Even talking about it would bring down the Government. So I want you to chair a committee of eminent industrialists to advise me.'

'Well, of course I'd be honoured...'

In such a way is the fate of nations decided.

Of course, this call hadn't come as a complete surprise. 'Dickie' Davis, the Brexit Secretary, had sounded me out the previous week. I was therefore ready to set out my conditions for taking on this patriotic service.

1. The other members of the committee would only be there for show. I'd call the shots.

2. No experts or civil servants putting facts in the way of some bold thinking.

3. A private jet at my disposal. (At least a Gulfstream IV: they can reach the Caribbean without refueling, and rebuilding links within the Commonwealth was going to be important.)

Once these minor details had been agreed, I was able to take up my historic role.

The less knowledgeable amongst you may ask, *why me?* Why should such an honour be vested in Sir Reginald Futtock, when it could have been any one of a dozen eminent and successful businessmen – or even Lord Sugar?

Let me explain.

If you look back over five decades of British industrial decline, you will see one name stands out. One name synonymous with our manufacturing achievements, with our triumphs in banking and financial services, and with our leadership in deregulation and privatisation. That name – I speak modestly – is Sir Reginald Futtock. From my beginnings at BAC, British

Leyland and Slater Walker, right through to the glory days at RBS, I have played a vital role in getting Britain to its current position on the world stage.

Then there is my wider contribution to the British economy. It is one of the duties that fall upon public-spirited industrialists such as myself that we are called to serve on the boards of a number of quoted companies for modest remuneration. And so I have had the privilege to help steer the destinies of household names such as BHS, Sock Shop and Woolworths, of industrial giants like Lucas and ICI, and innovative, mould-breaking technology businesses of the calibre of Sinclair, Marconi and ICL as they rode out to challenge the international goliaths.

This was the experience I offered to the Nation.

As Chairman of the Prime Minister's Committee for Escaping the European Union, my first task was obviously to come up with a better name for it. After all, PMCEEU is hardly the kind of dynamic, thrusting image that Britain will need to project in the years to come. So my first move was to bring in some top-notch design chaps to come up with a proper identity – serious, business-like, but with just a dash of patriotism. And £110,000 of consultancy fees later, we had our new brand: Brexit Solutions. Or BS for short.

Brexit Solutions has harnessed the intellect and ability of Britain's top people. Politicians like David 'Dickie' Davis and 'Mad' Mike Gove. Industrialists like Tim Spoons of the eponymous pub chain and technology wizard Noel Edmonds. Global trend-setters like Jim Davidson and Elaine Paige. Because with Brexit, we're all in it together, on the same sinking ship, even if some of us may have secured slightly better lifeboat accommodation than others.

At our first meeting, I explained that the task for the committee was to develop a Plan for Splendid Isolation. One that delivers the Prime Miniter's Brexit Vision – in which everything is radically different, unleashing the country's immense creativity and a new buccaneering spirit, and turfing out all the ghastly foreign people coming over here and creating jobs for us, while ensuring that absolutely everything is exactly the same as it is now.

This is our task, and we've gone at it with a will. Over recent months, our committee has heard evidence from experts in economics, international diplomacy, regional development, trade, innovation – you name it, we've listened to some ill-kempt academic going on about it. We've also heard from groups representing every aspect of Britain's life, from the Arts Council to the Zoological Society of London, about the impact that Brexit will have on their work. We've assembled thousands of pages of transcripts and thousands more of submissions from across the country and beyond.

And we've chucked all that in the bin.

Why? It would take far too long to go through it all, and in any case it's really a matter of politics, isn't it? We're out of the EU, and that's that. In any case, my own personal experience is worth far more than that of these so-called experts. Which of them has been responsible for handing out 31,000 redundancy notices in a single year? Or has actual experience of how you bribe a member of the Saudi royal family? That's the kind of practical skills we need in planning

Britain's post-Brexit Economic Miracle.

And it is the experience I now offer to you, the reader, as you too join this National Quest for Survival.

You too will want to know how Britain will fare in the future. How will we develop world-beating products and win back markets, while maximising short-term financial returns and not risking any serious money? How will we weld our nation together, all working for a common purpose, while ensuring that those at the top continue to receive their rightful rewards? This modestly-priced book holds the answers.

Drawing on my career, I will explain how Britain's future will look – and how you too can benefit from this catastrophe. For if every last one of us can profit from what is to come, if every last one of us in Britain can extract tax breaks, consultancies, directorships and monopoly pricing from these events, then, in a very real sense, there will be no actual losers.

This, then, must be our patriotic duty.

In the chapters that follow, I will explain how it was that Britain came to join the European Union, and why we left. I will review the main pillars of our economy – manufacturing, agriculture, technology, and so on – to show where the strengths and weaknesses lie. Then I will set out my Vision for Britain, our options for a new relationship with the bloody Europeans, and finally, the Plan itself. Then you will see – and I am speaking here to those amongst you who have yet to fully embrace the democratic voice of 37% of the British people to leave the EU – why we should all rally round the decision taken on 23 June 2016, as a new start for Britain. Or possibly for just England and Wales.

Since that fateful day, some have come to call me Mr Brexit. It is not a title I have sought or paid for (unlike my knighthood, or the Peerage promised in Nigel's first Honours list). But it is one I have accepted with humility. Today, as we throw off the shackles of international cooperation and embrace Splendid Isolation once more, we are at the edge of a chasm of unfathomable proportions.

Let us go forward together.

PART ONE:

THE GREAT DIVORCE

The European Menace

Over my long and fruitful career, I have had many European encounters (both metaphorically and, on some memorable sales trips, physically). I count myself pro-European in the usual British way. I like European food, wine and beaches. And I hate European toilets, electrical sockets and, of course, actual Europeans. So my support for Brexit – that is, for walking away from a project that has brought sixty years of peace and prosperity to Europe – is entirely consistent, and I resent the suggestion that I am motivated by petty chauvinism.

No, my chauvinism is on a much bigger scale. Europe, I have come to see, presents Britain with an existential threat: one where the only rational response is to leave the European Union without the faintest idea what will happen next.

What is the nature of that threat?

Well, of course that's more difficult. It's one of those nebulous, unspecific threats that is all the more dangerous for appearing to be the figment of the overheated imaginations of some cranks and fruitcakes. My good friends at the *Daily Express*, for example, are fond of reporting developments in the European Union under banner headlines such as IT'S THE END OF A THOUSAND YEARS OF BRITISH HISTORY. When you read the actual story, the facts don't always quite match up to the billing, but that doesn't mean that, deep down, they aren't on to something.

In response, you may have heard those fat-cat eurocrats, and their snivelling apologists in Britain, complaining about what they call 'Euro-myths'. They like to point out that so much reporting about the EU is simply wrong or even deliberately made up by unscrupulous journalists over a decent lunch to satisfy their editors or proprietors. And yet again, this is true: but misses the point. After all, who these days is interested in *facts?*

Take metric measures. When some market trader in a ghastly northern town insisted he wouldn't let his customers buy his fruit and veg in kilos, but only in pounds, he was – let's face it – being an annoying little twerp. But he was also the clay from which could be formed a shining example of British Pluck, the Dunkirk Spirit, and a dozen other of our national delusions – in other words, a Metric Martyr.

For this to work, you have to ignore the awkward fact that Mr Martyr was not being told he had to stop using good old British pounds and ounces. No, he was being told that if he displayed Imperial measures on his carrots and cauliflowers, he should *also* use metric ones. Which given we've been teaching our kids to use metric measures since 1971, is probably sensible.

But that matters not.

We didn't fight the French, the Spanish, the French again, and then the Germans twice so that some bunch of London bureaucrats could tell a greengrocer how to price his King Edwards. No, IT'S THE END OF A THOUSAND YEARS OF BRITISH HISTORY.

You might say to me – *hang on, Reg* (I think we're on those terms now, aren't we?) *hang on, Reg – surely there are bigger issues at stake than cucumbers and kilos? Surely the threat from the evil Brussels octopus runs a lot deeper than that?*

And of course it does. Much deeper. But this isn't the place to go into specifics. Just take it from me

Perhaps Nigel is wondering why, despite 40 years of European interference, we can still drink beer in pints.

that of course Brussels has a secret plan to crush Britain beneath its euro-jackboot and force us to eat garlic, throw donkeys off church towers and pickle our cabbage. The fact that they have waited since 1973 to begin to implement this plan only shows how subtle they are, and how dangerous the threat.

In this respect, it's important not to confuse the threat from Brussels with the ordinary, regrettable but inevitable march of progress. Take

Britain's fishing industry. It has been decimated in recent years. The obvious explanation is that in some way the EU's Common Fisheries Policy is a Spanish plot to come over here and steal our fish, and any attempts by our plucky, sea-dog fisherfolk to resist this second Armada has been met by the flying of Spanish jolly rogers, a blast of cannon-fire and some plank-walking, while hatched-faced Commission Inspectors look on laughing.

We might even contrast the surrender-monkey behaviour of our politicians with the stalwart, horned-helmet response of the Icelanders who in the famous Cod Wars of the 1970s fought off the gun-boats of a bullying European power, intent on stealing their fish. We might conclude our political class are intent on selling us down the river.

The reality is that Spanish fishing firms were bigger, invested more and were more efficient. Also, the reason the British couldn't use their national fishing quotas was that they'd sold most of them to the Spanish. No, the decline of British fishing was simply the operation of the Free Market, and if you think that should be interfered with in any way, then I'd kindly ask you to put this book down and more swiftly away before I do something we'd both regret.

Since the sainted Margaret took the British helm in 1979, our country has been a Free Market beacon and we're all the better off having closed our coal mines, decimated our industrial base and sold all our utilities to foreign investors. In fact, one of the few good things about the EU is that we've convinced the Commission that competition is a good thing and given them powers to enforce that across the whole of Europe. The last thing we want with Brexit is any interference in the right of the British business leaders to sell out their assets – and if necessary their workers, communities and country – to maximise shareholder value.

No, the danger to Britain lies elsewhere.

There was a time when Britain was truly Great, and everyone knew their place. Understanding where you fit in the hierarchy is tremendously important. It's a bit like a team in a game of rugger, isn't it? Everyone has their position, and a team where the prop turns up in the three-quarter line, or the hooker insists on telling the scrum half what to do, isn't going to win the match. And of course, everyone in the team has to do what the captain tells them. (If you didn't go to a proper school, or are a girl, don't worry: it's the same principal for Association Football or netball.)

In Britain, there have been occasions when amongst the ordinary members of the team (lets call them the workers) there have been some (let's call them socialists and revolutionaries) who have tried to change all this. And naturally, they've had to be suppressed with a reasonable display of force – one thinks of the Dragoons at Peterloo, the bayonets at Tonypandy or the riot police at Orgreave. More insidious was the idea that the team should choose the captain, rather than the captain being in charge because of their innate superiority, or the quality of their education, or by right of birth. Back in the nineteenth century, there was a loss of nerve amongst the natural providers of the country's captains, and democracy took root. Now democracy is of course a wonderful thing, and terribly British, but it has to be used wisely. Otherwise you start electing socialists.

Fortunately in Britain, we've developed a form of democracy in which there are checks and balances. This has served us well for nearly two centuries. When the voters have gone too far to the Left, then one part of our constitutional system, the popular press, has demonised the leaders of the Left until everyone sees the errors of their ways and casts their vote in a sensible, patriotic way again. And if the voters had ever gone too far to the Right, no doubt something or someone would have weighed in and sorted it out – but fortunately, that's never happened.

It's meant that Britain has, by and large, had the right kind of chaps in charge. People like me. People who can Put Britain First. Who understand that there are three things that constitute the National Interest: letting wealth-creators like me get on with it; letting us spend our wealth as we see fit; and letting us keep it that way for our children.

And this is what is threatened by Europe.

From the start, we British wanted one thing from Europe: a place to sell our shoddy goods, once the Empire had decided to give us the boot. Unfortunately, the Europeans wanted much more than that. They didn't just want to trade freely: they wanted to integrate their economies to make the idea of a future war in Europe unthinkable. They also wanted the people of Europe to come closer together, through social and political integration, and collaboration in areas such as scientific research.

The British approach was to ignore all of that, and

pretend that we were joining a trade block or Common Market. But that didn't work.

First we had the European Commission deciding that there should be EU-wide rules on protection in the workplace – the number of hours you can be expected to work, time off for sickness or injury, and so on. Their argument was that, in a Single Market, you had to have some basic standards, otherwise one country would allow their industry to screw the workers, and so undercut all the others. The other countries would in turn lower their standards, and before you knew it, the whole of Europe would be a kind of Victorian workhouse: what the Commission call a rush to the bottom. Absolute bunkum. (What you actually get with the removal of all employment protection is a rush to become the most lean, thrusting and dynamic economy in the world. Just look at China: no workers' right there, I can tell you, and all the better for it.)

We also had the Commission coming up with new product standards: rules for making things safer, or more efficient. Standards for fridges and dishwashers, cars and chemicals. Surprise surprise, lots of British products struggled to meet these so-called safety standards. As if a dose of pesticide or a piece of a toy lodged in a child's throat ever did anyone any harm.

What the Europeans have done on the environment is especially outrageous. No-one likes a drive in the countryside more than myself, but I mean, steady on! If we need a new airport or motorway in our green and pleasant land, then the British approach of having a public inquiry and then approving it anyway seems fine to me. Anything else could impinge on our ability to create wealth. But suddenly you had the European Commission saying we had to actually protect our wildlife, not just designate it as a Site of Special Scientific Interest and then build on it. A lot of decent chaps who wanted to invest in some rather tasty infrastructure projects were put to a lot of inconvenience, I can tell you.

Across a whole range of areas of our national life, this kind of wanton Euro-interference has got in the way of Free Enterprise and Wealth Creation. Health and safety. Employment rights. Discrimination. Women. Did you know it's actually illegal to ship hazardous waste to the third world? Unbelievable, isn't it? These are decisions we should be taking for ourselves, in Britain, in Parliament (or better still, in a discreet restaurant with the relevant cabinet minister).

So, in the name of the British People, as their recognised Betters, we are Taking Back Control. And that is what Brexit is all about.

How We Were Seduced

So if the European Union is such a danger to our country, how did we come to be embroiled in it in the first place? To answer that question, we need to go back to May 8th 1945. It was the day that I, Reginald Alexander Montgomery Spencer Futtock, was brought into the world. And at least as importantly, it was VE Day, when Victory in Europe was declared after the horrors of the Second World War. A day on which Europe lay devastated, its economic in ruins, unable even to feed its people; and Britain stood triumphant as one of the most powerful nations on

Our major economic rival in 1945.

earth, standing shoulder to shoulder with the USA and Russia.

Some may say that a comparison of our subsequent economic performance to that of the rest of Europe since that day is not very flattering to Britain. Certainly by the 1960s, there were aspects of British industry that gave rise to concern. Some might even go further, and say, *come on Sir Reginald, admit it, with the strikes and the collapse in the pound, Britain was so far down the toilet that it had gone through the sewage treatment works and been flushed out into the English Channel.* I say: well, you have a point, and it explains why we were all so keen to join the European Economic Community, as it then was. We were sinking, and the EEC was a welcome lifeboat.

Take aviation, which is where my own career began. In 1945, Britain led the world. We had a roll-call of famous firms and even more famous aeroplanes: the Hawker Typhoon; the Avro Lancaster; the de Haviland Mosquito; and most renowned of them all, the Supermarine Spitfire. That's to put to one side firms such as Airspeed, Blackburn, Fairey, Handley Page, Shorts and Vickers. In 1945, no-one would think of buying any kind of French plane (unless they had the bad luck to be French).

Fast forward to the 1960s, and things didn't look so good. De Haviland had come up with the world's first jet airliner, the Comet, but that had to be grounded after they showed a worrying tendency to fall apart in mid-air. Vickers built the VC10 to complete with Boeing's 707, but for various reasons (not unconnected with the main design criteria being that it should be able to operate from hot dusty airfields in Britain's African empire – not a big selling-point in the US) we only ever sold it to British customers and production soon closed down. Soon, the Americans had world markets sewn up.

It was the same story in steel, cars, trucks, motorcycles, railway engines, turbines: all the things we invented in the industrial revolution, or where we came to dominate world markets in the nineteenth century, were all sliding away from us. Soon, all that would remain were the tears in the eyes of a few nostalgia buffs.

Even in the new post-war industries like electronics, Britain was losing its way. We invented the computer, but IBM was the one that made the money.

The ICL 2966. When you bought a British computer, you certainly got a lot for your money.

So we have a picture of industrial decline, opportunities squandered, leadership lost. And lots of people ask, what went wrong?

This is sometimes explained as the Price of Victory. The line is that we took our immense wealth and superiority and spent it during the second world war on the cause of Freedom, while the French, Dutch and the rest were merrily collaborating away. Another view is that, had all our factories been bombed to bits by the RAF in 1945, as in Germany, we'd have started again by investing in the latest technology and coming up with world-beating products.

Another explanation is that Britain was too busy waging wars or crushing dissent in places like Korea, Malaysia, India, Aden, Cyprus, Kenya, and Palestine, and this kind of world policeman role doesn't come cheap. Meanwhile the Europeans were sheltering under the protection of NATO and investing in infrastructure, education and technology. Soon they were pushing us out of our world markets like the bunch of ingrates they really are.

Then there is the theory is that it was all down to the unwillingness of the City of London to invest in Britain's future, and particularly in manufacturing. Bunkum, of course. As I know from my time at Slater Walker, the City is only motivated by the desire to make money, and if there had been chances to make money in British industry, rather than just by stripping the assets, we would have taken them.

There are various other explanations that one hears from time to time amongst leftie intellectuals, about class, privilege, the country's education system, and so forth; but we can safely ignore all of those.

Whatever the cause, this decline forms an essential part of our story. Had Britain been strong enough to stand alone in the 1950s and 1960s, we would never have considered joining the European Union. When the founding members of the European Economic Community got together to plan their economic and political integration, we had an invite to the party. But on our side of the Channel we had a rather more grand vision of our place in the world, at the centre of three concentric circles: the Empire and Commonwealth; the Atlantic alliance with the United States; and Europe. Britain, uniquely positioned at the epicentre of these three spheres, could therefore carry on feeling immensely superior to all other nations.

However, there were some smart brains at work somewhere in Whitehall, for although on the surface we ignored the EEC, we also began to set up a rival organisation, called the European Free Trade Area. The idea was to gather together all the independently-minded countries of Europe that weren't under the control of the Soviet Union and get them to form a free trade bloc, but without the political integration of the EEC. We persuaded a whole rag-bag of countries, including Switzerland, Norway, Denmark and Ireland, to come on board.

This was fine, except that the EEC turned out to be something of a success, just as the evidence of our industrial weakness was becoming too much even for we British to ignore. Also, the German and French economies were growing far faster than our own, and as the internal barriers to trade amongst the Six came down, Britain was at a disadvantage in trying to get a slice of the action. So in 1962 we decided to sell our partners in EFTA down the river and join the EEC. Except that we also wanted to keep cosy with the US, and the French President, de Gaulle, who was rabidly anti-American, vetoed our application.

As the 1960s unfolded, the case for membership become ever-stronger – a mix of the success of the EEC and the worsening economic situation in Britain, with strikes, balance of payments crises and finally, in 1967, a humiliating devaluation of the pound.

Then, in 1969, a ray of sushine. President de Gaulle resigned, the French veto on British membership was lifted, and at last we could make our way to the European altar.

The European Commission: an overweening bureaucracy doomed to collapse since 1957.

The Honeymoon Years

Marriage is all about commitment, as I said to my fourth wife Tatiana as we enjoyed our romantic pre-nuptial signing ceremony. And when it comes to international relations, we British aren't very good about commitment. We keep eyeing up the bridesmaids, or having one last fling with our ex.

Within a year of joining, we were already talking about leaving again. The Labour Party was being torn in two over Europe, and the Prime Minister of the time, Harold Wilson, called a referendum on leaving the EEC as a shabby political stunt to help keep his divided party together. Not the best way to boost our influence and standing on the Continent!

It wasn't a surprise to me, though. From my very first job, at the British Aircraft Corporation, I'd seen how Britain was always in the awkward squad, thinking we knew best and in a majority of one. Back then, BAC was a thrusting, dynamic industrial powerhouse, formed when the main British aircraft firms, encouraged by the government, merged formed two new conglomerates: BAC and Hawker-Siddeley. The idea was that they'd have the scale to complete internationally with Boeing and the other big players.

Before I joined BAC, the company had decided that the future was in supersonic transport. The only problem was that the French were working on a similar design, and if both went ahead, neither would make any money. So BAC had little choice but to team up with Sud-Aviation. The result was Concorde.

At the time, the future was all about industrial collaboration with the Europeans. (Obviously, we would have preferred to hook up with the Yanks, but they didn't do collaboration. All they would offer was to buy us out, and they didn't seem to think we were worth much as manufacturers.) The way it worked was that various governments would get together and, like an arranged marriage, tell their national aircraft-builders that they were going to get hitched to Aerospatiale, or Messerschmitt, or Hawker Siddeley, or whoever was the chosen bride of the year. This was only fair enough, as the governments were the main customers – either for the military or because they owned the airlines.

Supersonic aviation was the place to be, so I was more than a little peeved to be put onto BAC's least glamorous project: following-up the humdrum but successful BAC 1-11 with 200 and 300 seat versions. The new BAC 2-11 / 3-11 was a sure-fire commercial winner – so naturally we planned to borrow most of the cash to develop it from the Government.

Our main British rivals, Hawkers, had joined a new European consortium to build a wide-bodied aircraft that could carry 300 passengers. This was a bit of a joke, as the idea of the French, Germans and British getting together to build an aircraft without losing gazillions of pounds was far-fetched, to say the least. They would also be going up against Boeing and Douglas, who had over 90% of the jet airliner business sewn up between them. Worst of all was the name: who on earth was going to buy a plane called an "Air Bus"?

Nevertheless, the British were one of the founders of Airbus, and committed money to the launch. Then the government got cold feet and pulled out. That meant the whole project was about to fold, so the Germans offered to loan Hawker Siddeley the money to cover their part of the Airbus design – the wings – so the thing could go ahead. Instead of being an equal partner in Airbus, with British government backing, Hawkers were in effect a sub-contractor.

At BAC, we looked on with a sense of quiet satisfaction. After all, we'd tried to keep clear of these Euro-entanglements. I could get on with drumming up orders for the All-British 2-11.

Meanwhile the engine-makers Rolls Royce had run into some marital problems of their own. They had always been tremendously sound on Europe – that is, happy to sell their stuff there but not interested in collaboration, and focused on breaking into the lucrative (and equally-important, decent, trustworthy, English-speaking) American market. To do this, they'd promised Lockheed to make a marvellous new engine for its Tristar, which was to compete with Boeing's 747 and the Douglas DC-10. This engine, called the RB211 (no, I have no idea why) was going to be part-funded by the British government. It also meant that there was no money left for the other engine Rolls was supposed to be designing – the RB207 which would have powered the Airbus.

Unfortunately, with money increasingly tight as

Ah, the BAC 3-11. It could have been the British Airbus, but it never left the drawing board.

the UK economy slowly fell to pieces in the late 1960s, the Government couldn't fund both the RB211 and the BAC 2-11. (I suggested we send in some invoices to the Ministry of Aviation anyway and hope they would be confused which 211 they were paying for, but as with so many of my best ideas, I couldn't win round my colleagues.) We hadn't enough firm orders to go ahead on our own, and so that was the end of the 2-11.

Worse still, the Airbus was actually going ahead.

That was bad for Rolls Royce. The European Airbus ended up with American engines. But it was also bad for BAC, as the 2-11 and 3-11 were cancelled.

This was mildly embarrassing for my good self, as I'd been one of those who'd snorted with derision at the idea of European collaboration. To try and save the day, we sped round all the European aircraft firms to see if we could bodge together a rival consortium. We recruited SAAB of Sweden, MBB of Germany and CASA of Spain. The design chaps drew some pictures. I came up with an exciting name for it – the Europlane! But Airbus was already up and flying by then. The

Europlane was doomed – and it was time for me to leave BAC for pastures new.

Something similar happened at a national level. Personally, I was in two minds about joining the EEC. On the one hand, the Common Market was part of a wider movement for European political and social integration, and we wanted no part of that. On the other hand, I knew that once the British were in, we'd be able to tell the rest of these excitable continentals what to do. Then we could drop this federal nonsense and get on with making money by plugging our tottering economy into the Franco-German economic miracle.

And so it proved. After we joined, and despite the economic turbulence of the 1970s, our economy began to recover. This wasn't all Europe, of course. We also had the bonus of North Sea oil. But by the 1980s, the two together had transformed Britain's prospects.

Realising that Europe was a complete money-tree as far as Britain was concerned, the next trick was to push our angle further. We got the Commission interested in competition and international free trade – that was one in the eye for the French, I can tell you. We got them going on completing the Single Market, so we could push our financial and professional services right across Europe. And then, with the fall of Communism, came the ultimate triumph of British policy: expansion to the East.

The starting-point for this was the reunification of East and West Germany. Although Britain tried to stop this, it turned out to be a success. So we effortlessly changed direction and instead began to insist that the

EU should welcome in all the countries of the former Soviet Bloc: Poland, Hungary, Bulgaria, Transylvania and so on. The reason for this was that all these countries would be natural allies for us. To them, we were a beacon of freedom and independence. Unlike the weaselly French, Germans and Italians, we'd never cosied up to the communists in Moscow. With their votes on our side in the European Council, we'd be in a position to over-rule the French and the Germans and make the EU do what we wanted.

For a few years, we were able to stymie most of the more progressive projects of the EU. We had the plucky Poles to weigh in if the Germans, French or Dutch got all wound up about workers rights or the environment; and if the Italians and Greeks came waving their bleeding stumps and asking for more money for regional development, we only had to point out how much this would cost when extended to the rest of Eastern Europe to frighten the German bankers, who after all were funding the whole show.

In short, the European Community worked just fine for us. A good place to do business, and a huge opportunity for us. But despite being in clover, our eyes began to stray.

Breaking Up

How was it that Britain came to find the reverse gear and start backing away from the continent, after more than forty years? The British, we're told, are wary of change. Uncertainty is bad for business. A whole raft of experts and celebrities had lined up to say we should stay in, from the Head of the Confederation of British Industry to former Captain of the British football side David "Posh" Beckham, together with the leader of every serious political party in Britain, and the Greens.

But as I have rather elegantly shown, Britain never really committed to Europe. We never forgot our first love – the British Empire. And we always had a bit of a thing for that big, busty broad, the US of A. The English psyche is, lets face it, riven with masochism. And that isn't just sand-filled sandwiches on damp and chilly beaches or standing for two hours with your nose in someone's armpit to get to work. It goes right back to childhood. If the Battle of Waterloo was won on the playing fields of Eton, then surely Britain's desire both to dominate and be dominated was kindled in the changing rooms afterwards. And without wanting to flog this psycho-babble too far, we never wanted a loving relationship with Europe as our equal. We always hankered after Nanny, who would come and make everything all right again. And who better than the US, who had done it in 1917 and 1941?

So the seeds of our exit were always there.

At the time we joined, the only people who were overtly against were some old Empire hands who dreamed of retaking India, and the Old Guard in the Labour Party. The former couldn't face the fact that Britain's day as a Great Power was over; the latter thought the whole thing was a bosses plot to make money and keep down the workers (which is what we hoped too — how wrong we were!)

There were also a few clear-eyed souls such as Enoch Powell who disliked the idea of handing over sovereignty to this supra-national body. But when the possibility of leaving the EEC was debated in Parliament, one rising young MP soon put him in his place.

> *"We could not be considering taking the country out of the Community unless Parliament were still sovereign."*

The words of Saint Margaret: and, for three decades, they seemed to me the last statement on the subject. In the 1975 referendum, 67% of the public voted to stay in. Every part of Britain (except for Orkney and Shetland) voted to remain. Anti-Europeanism remained the preserve of the Fruit and Nut Brigade.

Talking of which, some years back, my great friend and long-time Ludo partner Jimmy Goldsmith went completely off his trolley and developed a persecution complex. He became convinced that the EU was a conspiracy to destroy Britain, and he got so worked up about this that he moved to France and became a Member of the European Parliament. That didn't seem to bring him back to his senses, and he returned to form a new political movement, the Referendum Party. Its one demand was the Britain should hold another referendum on its EU membership.

Perhaps we should be grateful that Jimmy decided to take the political route. After all, he had a passing resemblance to arch-Bond-villain Ernst Blofeld, and had enough personal wealth to build himself an underground hideout, complete with death rays and henchmen in boiler suits, from which to plot world domination, had he so wished. As we have seen, the Referendum Party did get a wad of cash from Jimmy – enough to mail millions of British homes a video message from the Great Man, warning them of the peril and encouraging them to vote for his exciting

Sir Jimmy Goldsmith: a gain for British politics, a loss for SPECTRE.

new party. Predictably, very, very few of them did.

The same happened for many years with the UK Independence Party, which was the next lot of swivel-eyed obsessives to think the thing that mattered most in the world was that we had sacrificed some of our national sovereignty to be part of the EU, while being intensely relaxed about sacrificing some of our national sovereignty to be part of the United Nations, the World Trade Organisation, NATO, IATA and FIFA, to name but a few. UKIP warned the people and asked for their votes, and didn't get much response. Certainly they were a mile away from getting any actual MPs.

But then UKIP had a bit of a brainwave. People didn't really care about Europe. But immigration was going up, as the UK economy created more and more jobs; and people's blood pressure was going up, as the *Mail* and the *Sun* competed with the *Express* on lurid, foreigner-racist-scrounger, we're being swamped headlines. All UKIP had to do was hitch their wagon to concerns about immigration and they were off. They started taking votes from the Tories, who lurched to the Right in response, including demanding a vote on leaving the EU. Eventually, Cameron tried to steal their thunder by promising a referendum and the rest is history.

Like most right-thinking people, I assumed the British people would grudgingly vote to stay by a disconcertingly narrow margin. That was, after all, in everyone's interests. The handful of euro-believers would be delighted. The majority of pro-business types would be relieved. The Leave side would claim a moral victory, but not have to worry about putting

Leave: the cream of Britain's political leadership.

their extraordinary claims into practice. And best of all for them, they could carry on having the EU to hate and to blame for all the ills of Britain.

But the referendum campaign didn't go to plan. The Remain side was, in effect, all the most unpopular people in Britain, from Alastair Campbell to David Cameron, and backed by the massed political, business and banking elites, put into one room. And although Leave was hardly a beauty pageant, , they did at least offer the chance for Britain's greedy and ungrateful masses to stick it to someone.

Which they did. Bless 'em.

Of course, no-one had any idea what to do next. Nigel wisely followed my advice and began to dump all the ridiculous claims and pledges he had made during the campaign, such as "Lets give our NHS the £350 million that the EU takes each week". But that was just some light tactical repositioning. I was able to help him see that there was a much greater prize on offer: a very English coup.

Moving Out

We can all remember where we were when the result of the EU referendum was announced. (I certainly can, although the address I was at, the name of the young Latvian lady I was with and the nature of the equipment employed must stay confidential.) And that result was, let's face it, a bombshell. I and everyone I knew – chaps at the Club, our expensive Public Affairs consultants, my wife's tennis friends – were sure we would stay in Europe. After all, over the years, we'd all made piles of cash out of it. But the Great British Public decided otherwise. And once I'd showered, dressed ands returned to the Club, I was able to reassure my fellow Captains of Industry that all was not lost. The reason? I reminded them of Futtock's First Law of Business – one I'd learned when helping to save the British motor industry with the launch of the Austin Allegro: you can make just as much money out of a stupid decision as you can from a sensible one.

Obviously the decision to leave the European Union was monumentally short-sighted, and deeply harmful to our national security and prosperity. It had been brought about by political cowardice allied to the Xenophobic rantings of a clique of cranks, foreign newspaper barons and borderline-psychopathic businessmen, many of whom I now count as my closest friends. It would cost us almost unimaginable amounts of money, screw up the last few successful areas of our economy, and hand leadership in Europe to the French and the Germans. Russian Supremo Vladimir Putin would be rubbing his hands in glee, as would the Great Helmsmen of the Chinese Communist Party, ready to buy up Britain at rock-bottom prices.

But no matter. The very scale of the catastrophe would mean yet more easy pickings. And it was that very morning that I coined Futtock's First Law of Business Part B:

"The more stupid a decision, the bigger the potential profit."

And it was in this spirit that I put the call through to Nigel Farage and placed myself at his disposal. For by leaving Europe, we were setting sail on a new National Adventure − a return to the buccaneering days of the British Empire, when British ships carried British goods to British colonies where they were brought by natives under the watchful guns of the Royal Navy; and those same ships would return laden with riches acquired under very advantageous terms from local despots, again assisted by the Senior Service. That was to be our future. It would mean Britain would again be dependent for its very survival on the Few (not those RAF chappies, many of whom were foreign anyway) but on what I like to call the True Few − the Captains of British Industry, who at no small cost to themselves, create the wealth of the country and generously share a small proportion of it with the rest of you.

This was our hour.

I said to Nigel, on that historic morning, that I Was

With Him. Together, we would Make Britain Great Again. No more alliances with unreliable foreigners. No more collaboration across national borders. No, instead we were going to cosy up to the Yanks and get into bed with the Chinese and the Indians. That was our destiny.

The heart of the Futtock Vision, as it came to me that day, was The Coup. The great thing about the Referendum was that, at first, no one could then believe that the Leavers would win. Then, when it became clear that they had every chance of doing so, still no-one believed it. And so no-one, anywhere, had made any kind of plan for what would have next. And that was the vacuum that I at once stepped in to fill.

My simple idea was that, if we were going, then we should do it properly. There must be no shilly-shallying with attempting to keep a trade relationship – or any kind of relationship – with Europe. More important was the chance to remake Britain. For I could see that everything was up for grabs. Every law, every regulation, every spending decision, every policy. The decision was so monumentally crazed and destructive that literally anything could be proposed as a necessary act to save Britain from collapsing into a kind of post-holocaust dystopia in which the few ragged survivors would roam the streets eating dead rats or Pot Noodles.

So it could all go. Brussels. President Junkers. The Single Market with its annoying rules. Human Rights. The Greeks. Everything we didn't like could just be thrown to one side, like a scrunched-up cigarette packet flicked from the window of a Ford Transit.

Sometimes it's hard to recall the rapture of those days. Around us, the ghastly liberal elite was in mourning, weeping into their soya mochachinos, while decent upstanding British racists were finally able to emerge from hiding and exchange coded messages about national renewal and taking our country back. It was a time when anything was possible, from reintroducing leaded petrol to having a British GP. I have a document from that time that I treasure for just that reason – the first report produced by the PM's Committee on Escaping Europe (of which much more anon) reviewing what kind of relationship – if any – we wanted to our European ex.

It was slightly demeaning to have to compare the United Kingdom of Great Britain and Northern Ireland to a pile of frozen rocks that's greatest gift to the world is the paperclip (Norway), a semi-fascist island smaller than many a Russian oligarch's Scottish shooting estate (Singapore) or a vast, anonymous wasteland filled with dullards whose one saving grace is that they aren't American (Canada), but we live in difficult times and must not complain about our lot.

Of course, there have been some compromises since those heady days. But those initial weeks of work – ably supported by luminaries such as Bernhard Jenkin, Jakob Rees-Mogg and many others too unappealing to mention – laid the foundation for The Coup. There was at one point a great danger for the Exiteers – that people might start to wonder exactly where we were heading, or worse still, actually see where we were going and try their damnedest not to go there. Britain might have voted to leave the

Prime Minister

*Sir Reginald was keen
that you saw this before
your meeting with
Mr Farage*

RF 2.vii.6

The Prime Minister's Committee for Escaping the European Union

From: Sir Reg Futtock
Date: 1 July 2016

PRIME MINISTER

OUR FUTURE RELATIONS WITHE EUROPE: SOME OPTIONS

You asked for a briefing note on options for the shape of our future relations with Europe (you'll see I've dropped this 'rest of Europe' nonsense – Britain is an island, after all).

Norway

The Norwegians have twice been on the edge of joining the EU, and twice have pulled back from the brink. They were one of the founding members of EFTA, and joined us in applying for membership in 1962, 1968 and 1994, but each time a referendum narrowly kept them from joining. Since 1994, Norway has been something called the European Economic Area. It means they are part of the Single Market, except for foodstuffs, and this means they have to accept the free movement of workers, adopt thousands of EU Directives and also put up with the decisions of the European Court of Justice. They also have to contribute to the EU budget on pretty much the same bases as EU member states. There's very little appetite for applying for full membership a third time, or for leaving the EEA. So in short, these horned-helmet types seem to have the best of both worlds: but it wouldn't work for us. ECJ? Free movement? Nigel would have you on toast.

Switzerland

There are French Swiss. There are German Swiss. There are even Italian Swiss. Yet they all live peaceably together, despite every one of them owning an assault rifle. They also put up with huge numbers of overseas workers (well, not actually overseas, given that Switzerland is entirely landlocked, but you know what I mean) and have almost no crime or unemployment. Somehow, I don't quite see Britain turning out this way. Further, Switzerland is in EFTA and has an agreement with the EU that looks suspiciously like the EEA: Switzerland is pretty much in the Single Market and grudgingly accepts the free movement of EU workers. It also has to follow the decisions of the ECJ and it contributes to the EU budget. So again, it's not for us.

Canada

Although I have never knowing bought anything made in Canada, my researcher Camilla tells me that the EU is Canada's second-largest trading partner after the US. This may explain why the Canadians were so keen to strike a controversial Free Trade Agreement with the EU in 2016, even though this will hit some of Canada's sensitive industries, such as fishing (not salmon fishing, though, so that doesn't really matter to me). In this CETA deal, some but not all tariffs between Canada and the EU will be swept away, though they weren't very high in the first place, and Canada will also accept EU tourists and business people without requiring a visa. (Camilla, though a jolly bright girl, couldn't find out anything that the Europeans were giving up in return.) So even if we got a Canadian-style deal, it would make little difference. Or as the young people say, Meh.

Singapore

While Singapore doesn't have any special relationship with the EU, it is often cited as a shining example of how a small country can punch above its weight economically. Singapore is about the same size as the Isle of Wight, but unlike the Isle of Wight has a massive international profile, thriving economy and is not dependent on selling sticks of rock for its survival. Also, unlike the Isle of Wight, it is in the centre of a web of major trade routes and is also the entrepot for the industries of Malaysia and other south-east Asian countries. Exactly what this is supposed to prove about the future of Britain, which has a far larger population, very different economy and is on the other side of the world I fail to see. Fortunately most of the people who bilge on about Singapore haven't heard that it's a founder-member of ASEAN, the south-east Asia equivalent of EFTA, which is currently converting itself into a single market based on those pesky four freedoms.

North Korea

When people talk about Britain regaining its sovereignty by leaving the EU, we should look to the shining example of North Korea. No country has more sovereignty than this plucky slice of east asia. No-one tells them what to do. They have no trade agreements. They pay no attention to international law. They don't accept any foreigners. They are entirely self-sufficient. And I don't expect the citizens of North Korea spend much time buying mochas, bringing discrimination cases, trimming their facial hair or going to quinoa classes either. They have the firm smack of discipline. I'm not saying we should be like North Korea – each to their own – but we could learn a lot from them (if only we were allowed to enter the country to see how they do

EU, but that left our relationship with Europe up for grabs, and as you'll have seen, there was no shortage of options. And the closest parallel was with Norway, whose people were also split down the middle on membership. In their sensible, pragmatic, balanced, not-wound-up-by-borderline-racist-articles-in-their-national-newspapers way, the Norwegians had opted to have the closest possible relationship with the EU that stopped short of actual membership. Horror of horrors that Britain should accept anything like that!

The problem was that the Norwegian option meant we could stay in the Single Market, and so trade freely with the rest of the European Union. As an industrialist, I could see the superficial attraction of this. But I was soon helped to see that the Single Market isn't all it's cracked up to be. In fact, through Our Great New British Economic Miracle, we won't need the Single Market at all.

PART TWO:

BRITAIN'S ECONOMIC SCORECARD

The Single Market

My very good and much-misunderstood-by-City-regulators friend Jim Slater had a razor-like brain, and when he wasn't using it to speculate on the stock market or asset-strip undervalued British firms he liked to play chess. I recall that one day, as we returned from closing down another lame-duck enterprise, he started telling me about the world chess championship on in Reykjavik at the time between the bad-boy American Bobby Fischer and the cold, ruthless Russian Boris Spassky. Jim was disappointed that Fischer was threatening to pull out of the contest because the £50,000 prize money was not enough.

'But Jim,' I said. 'That's chicken feed. You could make it back in an afternoon by launching a lightning raid on a crocked engineering firm and selling off the assets to its competitors.'

'Quite right,' he replied. 'I'll do it.'

So Jim, who was a very generous chap, gave the

World Chess people another £50,000 and the match went ahead.

But then he got a call from the Bank of England. In his desire to promote the sport of chess, he'd forgotten about exchange controls. Unbelievable as it might seem, back then you were simply not allowed to take your hard-earned money out of Britain without getting approval from some jumped-up civil servant. Even going on your summer hols, you were only supposed to take £50 spending money. I mean, you could hardly go for a modest lunch at La Tour d'Argent for that, even back in 1974, when you could buy a small Northern industrial town for £500 cash. (What the ordinary folk of Britain had to put up with in those dark days I shudder to think. Probably filling their suitcases with tins of Spam to munch on the beach at Marbella. Fortunately I had an account with the Bank Keine Fragen Gefragt in Zurich, and Swiss Francs were easily converted into fines wines and *pâté de fois gras.*)

As it happened, Jim's donation became a matter of international prestige – the idea of Britain, supposedly one of the foremost industrial powerhouses in the world, not having the cash to fund some ridiculous chess match was just too shaming – and the thing went ahead. But it goes to show how far we've come since the sainted Margaret did away with exchange controls. Nowadays you can take, say, £1,000 spending money to ensure that you have a damn good time on your two weeks in Albufeira; and I can move, say, £260 million to the Bank of International Transactions in St Kitts and Nevis to take advantage of some attractive spot interest rates without anyone asking impertinent questions. So we are all winners.

Free trade is a bit the same. The more controls you have on what people can and can't do in business, the more we all lose out. And Adam Smith – who is, let's face it, a much more satisfactory prophet than that crypto-communist Jesus Christ – mapped it all out for us. If country A is better at producing, say, sausages, and Country B better at producing, say, potatoes, then it makes sense for A to concentrate on sausages, B on potatoes, and the two to trade so everyone can have plates of bangers and mash. But it isn't just trading your surplus – it's actually specialising in what you're good at that makes the world richer. It's our sacred duty to enhance the Wealth of Nations. If we all produce goods in our own country, and are prevented from trading with other countries, we all lose out: and that's a sin. That makes anything that gets in the way of international trade – tariffs, import duties, jobsworth customs officers, and so on – literally evil.

Right-thinking people in Britain have therefore always been supporters of Free Trade. It meant we could bring in corn from Canada to feed the millworkers of Manchester and Bradford during the industrial revolution, and if this undercut our own farmers, so much the better: they would lay off their peasants, who would then migrate to the cities and help keep wages down in the mills. Perfect.

But Free Trade on its own is not enough. It gets rids of duties and tariffs – essentially, taxes on things you import or export – but you still have all the fuss of clearing customs. And you can find yourself facing all kinds of hidden barriers to trade, intended to prevent producers in one country competing on equal terms with those in another. For example, back in the 19080s the French held up the invasion of Japanese cars by insisting that they all be taken to a testing centre up a moutain somehwere near Dijon to check they complied with French safety laws before they could be sold in France. This centre had one man with a clipboard to complete the checks on perhaps 100,000 cars a year, and he was liberally supplied with packets of Gaulois and encouraged to knock off work for a fag break whenever he liked. Result, something of a backlog at the centre, and everyone in France continuing to buy French cars.

(Of course, this is just the kind of admirably slimy behaviour one would expect from our French friends. Fortunately, Britain has so many individualistic ways of doing things, from driving on the left to having

Salute the hunble Type G BS1363 British plug: helping to keep foreign electricals from our island shores since 1947.

our own kind of plug, that we create plenty of import barriers without even trying.)

So if you want to go beyond basic free trade, and let businesses from different countries compete on a genuinely level playing field, then you need to do two other things: have a customs union; and have common standards.

A customs union means

that there are no customs controls between the member states. Anyone can ship anything to anyone without it being opened and poked about at the borders; and without having to fill in a load of bumph. This is obviously a good thing; but with it comes one other condition: you have to have a single set of rules for the external borders of all the members of the customs union.

Why? With Free Trade, you can agree different trade arrangements with different countries bilaterally. So you might do a deal with Canada to bring in corn free of tariffs, and in return have tariffs removed for British JCBs going the other way; but still charge tariffs on American corn.

Now those of you with more intelligence than ethics may have spotted a business opportunity here: namely, take American corn across the border into Canada, re-label it as Canadian corn, and export it to the UK without paying any tariffs. Naturally I've never engaged in this sort of thing myself (and anyone who suggests otherwise, particularly in respect of sugarcane exports via Guyana, will be hearing PDQ from my old chums at Carter Ruck) but I understand it can be very profitable. So with Free Trade, you still need lots of border checks to ensure that imports actually come from the stated country of origin.

That all gets very complicated when, instead of a simple commodity such as, say, corn or sugar, you have something more complex, like a car. That could have components made in lots of different countries, and all subject to different tariffs. So again you have to have a lot of paperwork to prove the extent to which that car may be subject to more favourable tariffs. But in a customs union, you do away with all that. The customs union negotiates trade deals and tariff rates as a single entity, and those rates apply to all imports and exports. So if you source the engines for your cars from outside the customs union, you pay the agreed tariff, and then after that you can put the engine in your car and sell it wherever you like within the customs union, without needing to pay any extra tariffs or fill in any paperwork. But it means that countries within the customs union obviously can't strike trade deals of their own with third countries.

A customs union does away with customs controls, but it doesn't do away with the French wheeze of using special rules or inspection regimes to restrict trade by the back door. For that, you have to agree a set of common rules. Once those are agreed – and legally enforced – you can have a genuine Single Market.

The legal enforcement bit is crucial because, if you let the members of the customs union police the rules, the risk is that those hidden barriers will creep back in. Also, even with the best will in the world (and will you get that from the Greeks? The Italians?) national courts will have different interpretations of the rules. So you need a court that can decide for the whole of the customs union, and if necessary override national courts. This is the same with the World Trade Organisation, which has a supra-national legal system. The only problem with the WTO is that it takes forever and is only really open to national governments. With the European Court of Justice, cases move a bit faster and the European Commission and even individual companies and citizens can bring cases. But the main difference with the WTO is that you don't need to go off to Strasbourg to bring a claim. Courts in Britain will dispense ECJ-style justice too. It's really only if there is a dispute on the interpretation of Euro-law that it has to go to the ECJ itself. So you can go to a Dutch court and use European law to help settle a case, and so ensure that the rules in one member state apply to every member state.

So, in short, a Single Market is better for business that just having free trade or even a customs union; but a Single Market can only work if you have a common external trade regime, standard internal rules, and a court to police those rules.

Now I think that's all pretty clear. But seemingly it's beyond many of my colleagues in government and in the media. The current Foreign Secretary Boris Johnson, for example, is fond of saying that Britain will have 'access' to the Single Market. I'm sure that, however badly he and Dickie Davis screw up the negotiations, we will have 'access' to the Single Market. Everyone has 'access' to the Single Market'. Guatemala has 'access' to the Single Market. But unless we accept the rules of the Single Market, we won't be 'in' it. The best we will have is a free trade arrangement with the Single Market, and we'll still face border inspections, tariffs and hidden restrictions on trade through EU standards.

Does this issue of standards matter much in practice? After all, if we make decent products, then surely the EU will still buy them? And we can safely leave the Single Market?

Guatemala: soon Britain too will have access to the EU's Single Market.

Let me give you an example from my time at British Leyland. Back then, one of the biggest pains in our corporate backside was our bloody American friends. We'd come up with a perfectly decent car: or at least, the TR7. We'd carefully research the US market. (Ah, that weekend in Vegas – where are Candi and Suzi now? Great days...) We'd even build a state of the art factory at Speke to assemble it. And then the US Department of Commerce would turn around and say, *sorry you guys, but the fenders on your rinky-dink little sports coupé are all wrong. We want big fenders like we have on our Cadillacs and Pontiacs.*

And we'd have to redesign the car and stick these massive great bumpers on it, and send one over for them to test. And they'd muck about for a year, and then say, *great, love your fenders, but we've got a new emissions regime – sorry we didn't tell yous guys sooner – and you're gonna have to change the pissy little engine you got in it 'fore you can sell it in the good ol' US of A.*

So we're tear the engine out, change the carburettors, stick it back in any try again. And they'd say *well that's fine and dandy, son, but over in Californ-i-a they're real pickled about their smog and you're gonna have to stick on a catalytic converter.* So it would go on, until even if we were allowed to sell the bloody things, it's at a loss. And this wasn't just on the TR7, but also the Jaguar (wrong kind of headlights, from memory) and the Range Rover (fuel emissions, crash testing) and in the end we gave up shipping Rovers over there entirely.

That's what we're going to face in Europe.

At the moment, the rules in the Single Market are largely developed in technical committees where the British have a seat at the table, a microphone, a little name plate with *Rouyame Unis* written on it, a carafe of water – everything you need for effective negotiations. We get to see all the documents in advance, we get to take the right Commission officials out to lunch, and if we are really up a gum-tree, we even have British Members of the European Parliament to get to wade in on behalf of UK Plc.

But in the bright new Brexit future, that all goes. Instead – if we're lucky – we'll have the same privileged access given to Norway. That means that the committees draft the rules, without Norway being there, even as an observer. Then, when all the deals have been done, and the rules are all ready to put into action, they send a copy to the Norwegians and ask them what they think. The Norwegians mull it over a bit, and then say: *ve haf som consherns* and start moaning about Article 4.9.3 or Annex II.1 or whatever. The EU listen for a bit and say to themselves – do we (a) reopen this bloody negotiation, which has taken years off our lives, or do we (b) tell the Norwegians that we're really grateful for their suggestions, but on reflection we're sticking with what we've got?

So in short, Norwegian influence is a great big *Ingenting.* (And you're smart enough to know what that means in Norwegian.)

Now I hear the cries of *Reg, what do you mean we'll have no influence? Doesn't this make Brexit a bit of a disaster for us?*

Stay Calm. When I was at Sandhurst, I was told that you should always concentrate your forces where you are making a breakthrough. Follow up on success. And the flip side of that is, when things aren't working, ayou should give up and try something else.

So it's time to face some facts about the European Union.

The idea of joining was that we'd have access to this vast market, and we'd be able to sell our goods and services and we'd make a lot of money. But this was based on the idea that Britain made stuff other people wanted to buy. And the evidence I've seen in my long and illustrious career is, we don't. Or rather, not enough.

Yes, there's my good friend James Dyson and his hairdryers or whatever. Nice design – although not actually made in Britain.

Then there's whisky. Bloody good, and people buy it all round the world. But not exactly innovative, if you know what I mean. Not *cutting edge*.

Then there are the diggers made by JCB. Some of them are even made in the UK. But JCB is a bit of a one-off, because unlike almost every other large business in Britain, it's family-owned. No reliance on the City of London. No risk of being suddenly snapped up by the Japanese or, God help us, the Qataris. So JCB is not a model it's easy to replicate.

So there are some successful British businesses. But not nearly enough to take advantage of the scale of the European market. Why? Because it's so rare in Britain to get the design, the finance and the business organisation all lined up at one time.

When I was at British Leyland, we had factories in Belgium and Italy, making cars for the European market. Yes, that's right: a British firm owning factories in Europe making British cars to sell to continentals.

Well, they are of course long gone. But part of the rationale was that we'd sell even more once we were in the EU. Unfortunately, the British cars they were making just weren't that good. In Italy, we had to get an Italian to redesign the supposedly-iconic Mini so that people would buy it. And the French preferred these British-Italian cars because of the styling and because they were better built. Yes, appalling isn't it: even the Italians could put a car together better than we could.

And because there's so little British manufacturing left, we get rather a rosy idea of what it can do.

Firms like Rolls Royce (the aero-engine side, not the car company that we sold to the Germans long ago) really can beat the world. But again, there are so few of them. They are the survivors – lean, tough, battle-scarred veterans. But particularly after dear Maggie let so many firms go to the wall in the 1980s, and a lot more either failed or were sold overseas since, they are few and far between. So many great names have gone: I know, because I worked for many of them. Had they survived, they might have thrived in the Single Market. But they didn't, so the Single Market – from Britain's point of view – was never really about manufacturing in the traditional sense. It was partly about selling things assembled in the UK but designed elsewhere – cars, computers, televisions and so on; but mostly, it was about selling services.

What Britain is still good at – or let's be a bit more accurate, and say what South-east England is really good at – is financial and professional services. In the City of London, and spreading through the West End, are the businesses that really keep HMS Britain afloat. Hedge funds. Merchant banks. Derivitives traders. Commodity dealers. Shipping lawyers. Security consultants. Investment analysts. Re-insurance brokers. You don't know what they all do. I don't know what they all do. If they're making serious money, they certainly don't want us to know what they do. But what we do know is that they make vast profits and pay themselves enormous salaries and bonuses, and some of that finds its way to the rest of the country.

These people also operate across Europe – particularly in banking and insurance. It means

London can go into places like Warsaw and Bucharest and compete with the local banks, using their size and depth of skills to clean up. They can even switch people from one European capital to another without worrying about work permits or whether they have the right professional qualifications. This is all guaranteed by the Single Market, under which – as well as the free movement of goods – you also have free movement of services, capital and workers.

The flip side of this is that workers from the rest of Europe have the right to come and work in Britain. After all, it would be a bit difficult to sell to the Poles the idea that Brits can come and take their jobs in banking and insurance, while Poles can't come and work here. And if you have a relatively weak economy, the people may actually be your greatest asset (unlike in Britain, where saying people are our greatest asset is just a shop-worn bit of industrial relations blarney).

So here's the essential problem of the Single Market. It works best if you are good at growing things, or making things. And as we shall soon see, the UK doesn't have much spare land for agriculture, and has a bit of a problem with manufacturing.

Manufacturing

We've already seen that, in my lifetime, Britain's aerospace industry has gone from world-beating to also-ran, so that even our jet fighters are either made jointly with the Europeans or bought off the shelf from the Yanks. To rub salt in the wounds, other nations – even the Swedes – have managed to stay in the game.

This wouldn't be so much of a worry if aviation was a on-eoff. But it's the same story right across British manufacturing.

In 1945, Britain was awash with famous car manufacturers: Austen, Bristol, Jaguar, Riley, Triumph, Morris, Rover, Hillman, Standard, MG, etc, etc, while the French had just three: Renault, Citroen and Peugeot. Today, there are no volume

Come on, Swedes, this is our job! You stick to meatballs and flat-pack furniture.

car manufacturers left in British hands, and the French have three: Renault, Citroen and Peugeot. Of course, we still make cars here. Exclusive marques such as Bentley and Aston Martin for people like me, and Nissans and Fords for people like you. That's fine for making sure there are at least some jobs in benighted parts of the country like Sunderland and Luton, but all the really clever design stuff tends to happen elsewhere. And if there are any nasty decisions to be made, those will be taken in another country, potentially on the other side of the world (or more worryingly, in France: as when Renault bought Hillman, scrapped the marque and then closed the factory). Not a comfortable position for UK Plc. (Or for Vauxhall, now it's owned by Renault.)

Even in the new post-war industries like electronics, Britain has lost its way. We invented the computer, but the last firm in Britain to make computers – ICL – was sold to the Japanese long ago (and though I was a director of ICL at the time, there was nothing I could do to stop this: after all, the interests of the shareholders are sacrosanct). We were the first country in the world to build a nuclear power station, but it is the French who generate 80% of their power through nuclear; and the British who have had to grovel to the Chinese to fund the construction of a French-designed power station at Hinkley Point.

When I joined British Leyland, it was the largest car manufacturer in the country and employed 170,000 people. We were still Britain's largest exporter. BL also had by far the best executive dining facilities of all the major UK manufacturers, and you could also get some great discounts on their range of sports cars. There was a lot of international travel, with the added advantage that no-one actually expected you to sell many cars at the end of it, because of course the French, Germans and – increasingly – the Japanese made better cars at a cheaper price. They had gone down the route of advanced engineering, quality control and customer service. Our alternative – nailing bits of walnut veneer on to the dashboard – just couldn't compete.

My own role at BL was as part of the team bringing in a new mid-sized family car, the Austin Allegro. The design team had come up with a futuristic look, a kind of sharp-edged wedge, very fashionable. I had to veto that. The problem with fashion, I told them, is that it soon goes out of fashion. And where are you then? Paying good money to retool the production line. That's why I pushed for a redesign that would be 'timeless'. It meant we could keep selling the thing for years without an expensive update.

It made the new Allegro a bit bloated – with their typical Scouse wit, the shop floor at Longbridge christened it the Flying Pig – but by reusing the engine and making the thing 'timeless' we'd made the whole thing more profitable.

What really got the Allegro out there was the advertising: my own particular contribution. I think it's fair to say that it still turns heads.

We sold over 650,000 Allegros, which is pretty good going, I'd say. I've sometimes had my leg pulled by my old friend Jeremy Clarkson about my role in launching the Allegro. Jeremy and I go back a long way – he was the man who introduced me to embroidery, which is a

One of my better days working at BL!

very relaxing past-time after a hard day sacking people – and I can take a bit of raillery. Anyway, whenever there is a list of the nation's most well-known cars, the Allegro is always top of the list, which shows that ordinary people – not the sneering metropolitan elitists who watch Jeremy's TV shows – liked it.

Anyway, the Allegro was launched and British Leyland was saved. For a bit. But by then, I was thinking of pastures new. In business, you don't want to stay in any one firm too long. For one thing, you start having to take responsibility for your decisions. For another, it shouldn't take more than a couple of years to use up all the available perks, and fill up your address-book with useful contacts. Then it's time to jump ship. But do this too often, and even HR professionals might start to wonder if you are quite the right thing

But I'd seen at BL, and at BAC before then, that manufacturing was a mug's game. First, you had to have workers, who were a complete pain – worse even than customers. Second, no-one was paid nearly enough. With the cost of wine, salmon and Italian suits rising every year, it was hard to make do. Plus I'd gone and got married to Margot, there was son and heir Horace on the way, and fees at Harrow were becoming rather stiff.

Fortunately, one of my predecessors at BL, Jim Slater, had gone to the City and shown us a new way of thinking. The future wasn't about running businesses, but trading in them – not making things, but the Service Sector.

The Service Sector

Services are the great success story of the last thirty years. While manufacturing businesses have been dying off like mayflies in June, our banks, insurers, accountancy and legal firms, management consultancies and commodity traders have been raking it in. The City of London has become Europe's financial centre, and as Europe has expended to the east, and the German economy in particular has forged ahead, London has risen on a tide of fat fees.

So if manufacturing is not going to keep Britain's afloat in the years to come, are we right to turn to services as our saviour?

Up to a point. There will be winners and losers. But if you really want to know what is to come, it's time for me to reveal how services actually make that money — something that, as a former director of the Royal Bank of Scotland, I'm well-placed to do.

Most of us, most of the time, are pretty price-conscious. We might think that paying someone £10 an hour to iron your shirts or mow your lawn is pretty generous, and that a plumber who charges £50 an hour is ripping us off. But when it comes to selling airlines and water companies, different rules apply. The bankers, lawyers, consultants and accountants will cheerfully ask for £1,000 an hour and more, and get it too.

You'll be familiar with the principle from your own experience in buying a house. Unlike lawyers (who usually bill you by the hour) and surveyors (who will survey your house for a fixed fee) estate agents don't charge for the time and effort they put into selling your house, but instead charge a percentage of its value. Why? There's no logic to it. Their costs – taking some photographs to make your mean little semi look like Buck House and putting a signboard up outside to advertise themselves – are the same whatever the value of the property. Partly, of course, because they don't actually spend much time selling it, and it would look bad on the timesheets if you could see just how little effort they put in. But more than that, estate agents know that the surest way to make money is to hang on to other people's: or as the mediaeval merchant princes used to say: *Stickie fingeres maketh proffits.*

Once you're dealing in hundreds of thousands of pounds, people don't start questioning whether the brash boy or girl in a sharp suit who sold it for you is worth their 1% or 2% fee. the bigger the amounts of money you're handling, the easier it is to justify creaming a nice little earner off the top.

Retail banking has some of the same looking-glass economics. Unless like me you have an account at a real bank (Coutts, Hoares, and so on) you probably enjoy what is laughingly called 'free banking'. That is, as long as your account is in credit, you don't have to pay for all the services the bank provides for you. How nice of them, you might think. Or more likely, you'll have assumed that the Power of the Consumer is making them fight for your business, even if they can't make any money on it.

Oh dear.

You only have to open a newspaper to see the fallacy. There are the adverts pleading with people to bring their accounts to the High Street banks. Even offering cash bribes – £50! £100! – if you will convince your friends to switch. Why do they want to spend so much on finding more customers for a product they give away for free? Well, for one thing they can make money by screwing you royally if you drop into the red. They issue the warning letter (say, £30), apply the unauthorised overdraft fee (£50) and the punitive interest rate (10% above base rate), and in one day they've made more money than they would have got for an annual fee on the account.

But that's just bread and butter to a High Street bank. What they really want is the chance to flog you financial services, because these are expensive products which very few people understand, on which you can charge enormous hidden fees and therefore cover the enormous losses sustained by incompetent lending in the third world, and still leave some over to pay yourself a bonus sufficient to send Josh and Poppy to a decent school. So the price you pay for your free bank account is a letterbox full of offers for loans, pensions, trusts, bonds and insurance. And, being weak and greedy, you fall for them.

And these two ways of making money support each other. Bleeding you for more savings, premiums and the rest make you more likely to go overdrawn. And they can then keep charging you because you didn't read their warning letter. Why? Because you assumed it was yet another mailshot trying to get you to buy life assurance you don't want, or to take out a personal loan you don't need.

Of course, running a bank has overheads. One of those is advertising. If you are an unprincipled and greedy moneylender, it's essential you use some of the cash you generate from your dim customers to pay for endless slick adverts about how much you are the Nation's Local Bank, There for the Journey, Listening, Making Your Business Dreams Come True, and similar horseshit – literally, with Lloyds black horse crapping out nonsense about wanting to help you move into your first home or start your dream business, while busily repossessing homes and closing

Oh look, your friendly High Street bank has sent a horse to watch over the birth of your child. How lovely. They must really care. And if you fail to keep up your mortgage repayments, don't you worry. They won't put you and your newly-born child on the street. Do you know what frightens me most? You people fall for this stuff. Yes, you do. At least, as my bank is based on the sun-kissed island of Tequila, I know that my bank manager is motivated solely by the prospect of grotesque cash bonuses. Frankly, I'd be worried if they weren't.

down businesses to cover up for their own lending blunders.

Because while running a bank is a licence to print money, it can also be a licence to destroy it as well – on a monumental scale.

When I joined Royal Bank of Scotland as a non-executive director, it had some pretty impressive statistics. It had operations in in 69 different countries, 200,000 employees and £2.2 trillion of assets – more than twice that of the UK economy.

When I stepped down a few years later, the numbers were equally dramatic: 90,000 redundancies, losses of £24 billion, and a £45 billion bail-out from the UK Government. Essentially RBS, like all the other banks, had decided to take some absolutely stonking, eye-watering, mind-bending risks with the money we had been given to look after. The reason was simple enough: the safer a loan, the less money you make – while big, ballsy, risky loans come with far bigger profits. And profits mean bonuses for the directors and the senior managers. So naturally, banks just made more and more risky loans.

There are some basic checks and balances in banking. For example, have you ever met the person you are lending to? Are you sure they exist? Do they have any assets? Or a track record in paying back the money they borrow?

But these can get in the way of developing a really tasty loan portfolio. The kind where you can make it so complicated that even other commercial bankers don't understand what it is, but certainly don't want to miss out on the latest wheeze for jacking up profits to new highs.

Looking back on the events at RBS, I do have some mild regrets. Clearly, the 98% fall in share price is unfortunate. The loss of £24 billion was the largest in British corporate history (though that had the advantage of over-taking the previous largest-ever loss, sustained when I was ever-so-slightly associated with Marconi).

As a non-executive director, it has been put to me that I have some small share in the responsibility for this. But that entirely misunderstands the role of the non-executive. Company boards have two kinds of directors: those who are employed to run the business day to day, and those who have no direct, executive function but instead take an overarching supervisory role, and for which they receive a modest fee: say, £100,000 for working one day a week.

Non-execs are appointed by the rest of the Board, who want someone who will provide wider experience and constructive challenge, and useful contacts, but who won't rock the boat. Why? Well, if the boat is sailing along happily, there's no need; and if the boat is being tossed about on stormy waters, or even worse, beginning to sink, then having some extra people rocking it from side to side is hardly helpful, is it? And if your non-execs are going to have the right kind of experience, and the right kind of contacts, then inevitably they will be directors or other, similar companies to your own. Some characterise this as an old boys' network. I see it more as having a cadre of suitable candidates who all happen to know each other and play golf together.

How will they be independent, you might ask? But you don't really want your non-execs to be too independent, do you? I mean, if they were the sort of people who believed in linking executive pay to the wages of junior staff, or other socialist nonsense peddled by the likes of Oxfam, then by definition they wouldn't be director-material, would they? The clue's in the name, isn't it?

No, the ideal non-exec is one who raises their voice if they think there may be a problem, but is soon reassured by some bland statements from the management and a fact-finding trip to one of the company's more agreeable locations; ideally in the Cayman Islands.

The RBS story might lead you to two conclusions. First, that maybe Britain shouldn't rely too much on services, which can go wrong just as badly as manufacturing; and second, that a bit more regulation or supervision would be a good thing.

Wrong. And wrong.

Dealing with supervision first. Who is to provide that supervision? The Treasury? The Bank of England? Parliament? In other words, bits of government that are full of people waiting their turn to take up directorships or other roles in the businesses they are supposed to oversee. And don't forget that spectacular losses are often preceded by spectacular profits – but we don't hear so much about those, do we (mainly because we try and squirrel them away in various tax havens, but no matter). No, it's clear that chaps in the City are best placed to regulate themselves, with a very light touch supervision from the Treasury.

And yes, of course we can't rely on services – but they offer three great advantages over manufacturing: the jobs are nearer the Royal Opera House; there are more chances for excess profits, and they employ far fewer union-type troublemakers. If that isn't a sound foundation for Britain's future, I don't know what is.

Technology

In the Brave New World of Brexit, one of the things we're going to need is lots of multinational companies who are big enough to invest in the next generation of products. Otherwise we'll fall further behind and people like you will be out of a job. I saw for myself this happen in aerospace, where the British players were just not big enough to put jet aircraft in the air on their own. It was the same with cars, where Rover couldn't afford to develop new models to compete with real mass-market firms such as VW, Nissan or Renault. And the great hope of British computing, ICL, long ago cashed in its 'chips'.

Nowhere is the modern need for vast resources more clear-cut than in technology. Britain has a huge research base. We have more Nobel prize winners in science per head than any other country. We have some great innovative start-ups and tech firms. But none of them have grown up to join the ranks of Microsoft, Apple or Cisco. When they get to a certain size, they either find they don't have the financial resources to exploit their position globally; or a bigger rival snaps up their shares on the stock market. Either way, it's the same outcome: they become part of a larger, non-British set-up.

ARM was a British firm, based in Cambridge, that made the chips that form the brains of most of our electronic devices, including the Apple iPhone. But ARM is now part of the Japanese company Softbank.

And Autonomy wrote cutting-edge software that was used by thousands of companies around the world to manage their ever-growing archives of data: but Autonomy was bought out by the American firm HP (a really diverse conglomerate – apparently they make everything from computer printers to bottles of sauce).

We need to change this. And my experience on the board of Britain's largest electronics firm shows how it can be done.

For my younger readers, the initials GEC won't mean much. But for thirty years, there was hardly a piece of electrical kit installed in Britain, from fridges to power stations, telephone exchanges to radar, that didn't come from a GEC factory. It was already a significant business when a young chap called Arnold Weinstock came in as CEO. Weinstock's family were immigrants but despite this he built GEC up to be Britain's second-largest manufacturer after ICI. The recipe was simple: cautious expansion in sectors that GEC knew and understood, backed up by really close financial management, where the team at the top knew where every penny was spent, and some astute strategic alliances with decent firms such as GEC's French rival GCE. By the time Lord Weinstock, as he had become, was due to retire in 1997, GEC had £3 billion cash in the bank, was making profits of £1 billion a year, and employed 250,000 people, mostly in Britain. Most importantly, the shareholders had enjoyed higher dividends every year, and their shares had gone up in value enormously over the three decades of Weinstock's tenure.

I was appointed to the GEC board at about the time that Lord Weinstock was thinking about retiring. Naturally, I was one of the people to whom he turned to when the question of his successor came up, and I was able to give him the benefit of my many years experience of sizing up people. We were standing outside the boardroom of GEC's rather shabby and cramped offices – Weinstock didn't understand the need for corporate headquarters to radiate a certain glamour and prestige – and I looked down on the funny-looking, rather scrawny chap (no prop forward he!) and was delighted that I, Sir Reginald Futtock, was here to do my bit to steer him in the right direction.

'Arnie,' I said. 'There's only one man for the job. George Simpson.'

'But what has George Simpson ever done except sell Rover to the Germans for far more than it was worth?' he asked.

'Exactly,' I replied.

Well, I could see he wasn't convinced, but I was not alone in backing the Simpson for GEC campaign. The whole of the City was behind it. Why? GEC might be the most astonishing success story of the post-war British economy. But it was dull. Dull, dull, dull. Dull. Lots of profits, employment, stability, export success, research and innovation. But no deals. No fat fees for one's colleagues in the City. None of the excitement of smoke-filled rooms, secret negotiations, attractive share option packages and the rest of it. And George Simpson was the deal-maker of the day.

Corporate deal-making is a bit like giving steroids to an athlete. It might have some small negative long-term effects (heart disease, crumbling joints, obesity) but in the short-term it turns you into a winner. With George Simpson at the helm, the share price would be going north at a rate of knots.

Arnie gave in and the appointment was made. George embarked on a bewildering series of deals, buying and selling huge chunks of GEC. Industrial engineering, train manufacturing, shipbuilding, heavy electronics – all were sold. He used the money raised to invest in the US. His strategy was to get out of European alliances and make GEC – or Marconi, as he decided to rename it – the world leader in its chosen field of telecoms and communications equipment. In one year he spent £4 billion on buying US businesses.

It was difficult for me, as a non-executive director, to keep track on it all. So I decided not to bother, and just sat back for the ride. After all, GEC's share price

Boring old GEC, making things people needed.

had shot up, and it must only be a matter of time before my own modest director's fees were reviewed upwards. Not for personal gain, you understand: a company doing battle with the giants of the telecoms industry had to pay top whack. It was a matter of prestige.

It was around the time that some clever chap discovered the internet, and as everyone piled in to get a share of the action, any company remotely connected to telecoms and IT stood to gain. Marconi's share price peaked in 1999.

We all knew that one day the tech bubble would burst. That's the point of capitalism. The people with the inside knowledge and connections make money on the way up. They let in the little people and the idiots (such as most pension fund managers) to have a share of the dessert. Then the smart chaps slip out and get in the taxi, leaving the dunces to pick up the bill when the stock market plummets.

Sure enough, by 2001, Marconi's share price had fallen from £12.50 to 4p each.

The old, boring, stodgy GEC wouldn't have been so strongly affected. After all, if telecoms went down, there'd still be military kit to sell, or new trains to build, or a power station project, lots of it on long-term, government-backed contracts. But we'd sold the military side to BAe, and the trains and power stations to Alsthom.

Lots of other businesses around the world were suffering too. Intel's share price went from $42 to $16, and Apple's from $52 to $14. But for Arnie, who was still Marconi's President Emeritus, that only rubbed salt in his wounds. We had rather a tense board meeting. He pointed out that, if we'd still had the £3 billion in cash that he'd left to George Simpson, they could have stepped in and bought up an immense range of valuable assets at a knock-down price, knowing that they would one day recover their value. It would – according to Arnie – have made GEC the leading telecoms manufacturer in the world, while still meaning we had the engineering and defence businesses as well.

But I had an answer to that.

'Arnie,' I said, in sorrow more than anger. 'You can't cry over spilt milk.'

That left him speechless, I can tell you.

It was the last time we met. I decided that I needed a new direction. And Marconi, now worth less than £50m, was hardly a significant enough firm for my talents. So I decided to have a chat with some of the chaps about what was out there, and before I knew it, was on the board of that venerable and cautious bastion of traditional financial rectitude, the Royal Bank of Scotland.

But as I left Marconi's glittering new West End headquarters, weaving my way around the removals people taking out the lavish furnishings, I reflected on what I had learned.

First, that you can't succeed without taking risks.

Second, that risks can go very badly wrong.

Third, that the obvious answer is to make sure the risks you take are someone else's: their money, their jobs, or their legacy.

And so on that very day, in the limo heading

crosstown towards RBS's headquarters, I coined Futtock's Seventh Law:

> *"Make your money out of other people's risks,*
> *never your own."*

And for the post-Brexit world, this could be the most important insight of all. Brexit may be an exciting opportunity. It may open up huge new markets for us. But even I can't pretend there aren't going to be risks. Inflation, unemployment, higher taxes, declining public services. The only way to avoid those risks would be to stay in the EU, and that we will not do.

So I say we must face up to those risks, not be afraid of them, perhaps even embrace them. But above all, make sure they fall not on myself or those close to me, but on those best able to bear them. Just as the fall of GEC was borne nobly by the small shareholders, the pensioners and the 31,000 people who lost their jobs, so too the risks of Brexit must and will be laid squarely upon the ample shoulders of the brave, stalwart, hearts-of-oak, never-say-die, Dunkirk-spirited ordinary People of Britain.

The Creative Industries

The creative industries are vital to Britain's future. So it's a shame that they are exclusively populated by self-obsessed freaks, underachieving layabouts, two-faced venomous harridans, deviants, fruitcakes and brand consultants. If their hair isn't dyed cobalt blue or magenta, then they spend too long on sculpting their facial hair or on choosing what brand of cigarette to accessorise with their motor scooter. They are invariably gossiping, browsing through Tumblr, playing table football or redesigning their personal websites when they should be working; and they cannot even order a cup of coffee without turning it into performance art of soy and macchiato.

But in an age when Britain no longer manufactures merchant ships, motorbikes, trains or trucks, it's some consolation to know that we make the best adverts, corporate identities and installation art in the world.

So how do these ghastly people with their European mind-sets and undisciplined habits come to be a cornerstone of post-Brexit prosperity? Simply that, in the right hands, they have tremendous money-earning potential. WPP is one of the few consistently profitable British firms. Run by a hard bastard called Martin Sorrell, it has taken on the Yanks and the Frogs and won. Money pours back to London from advertising agencies and design bureaus around the world. Sorrell's genius is to take this unpromising raw material and turn it into creative gold, and those who whine at his pay packet – when I say 'packet', he's paid £769,231 a week, so it would be more like a pay suitcase, but that's the worth of the man – are simply the kind of knockers this country would be better off without.

And to be fair, within the catch-all of the creative industries are in fact some decent people. Andy McNab, for example, with his cheery takes of derring-do in Afghanistan and Iraq is part of it: all those paperbacks shipped to the States bring in much-needed foreign earnings. It's the same with British films about how much better everything was in the past. Then there are musicians such as my very good friend Mike Hucknall and his singing concerts; those wonderfully funny and inventive Mr Bean films through which dear, dear Rowan has cornered the Albanian market; and it's all good for UK Plc.

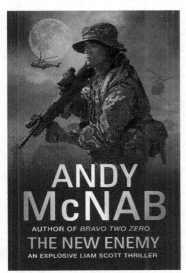

Earning hard currency for Queen and Country.

The prospects for the creative industries post-Brexit are really remarkable. As everyone knows, adversity is a spur to the creative instinct. Painters starving in their garrets and all that. And post-Brexit, one thing we won't be short of in Britain is adversity. We'll have simply thousands of artists, writers, film-makers, photographers, sculptors, musicians and actors, sound engineers and set designers, all wondering where their next meal is coming from. If that doesn't get the creative juices flowing, I don't know what will.

But perhaps the greatest contribution that the creative industries will make to Brexit is in helping to sell it. After all, there will be some dark days ahead. The decline in national wealth. The loss of influence. The feeling that we've become the Nobby No-mates of Planet Earth.

And we'll need something to get us through those bad times; when simply blaming the EU or foreigners in general is not enough. When, damn it, some people might even begin to ask why on earth we decided to leave the EU in the first place.

That something is bullshit. And if it's bullshit you need, creative are just the people to turn to.

We'll need bullshit to help sell Britain to the world. And bullshit to help sell Brexit to the British people. Or rather, to convince them not to rise up with pitchforks and burning torches against their natural leaders when they discover that Brexit isn't quite what they wanted but there's no right of return.

We've been to see some of the leading advertising and marketing people and already there are some pretty exciting ideas being kicked around.

For several years, we've been promoting British exports using a remarkably clever and effective slogan: "Britain is Great". In case it doesn't strike you straight away, what those immensely creative design people have done is taken "Great Britain" and "riffed" it by moving the "Britain" up ahead of the "Great" and slipping a cheeky "is" in to give it a unique twist that also says something terribly profound. Because Britain *is* Great, isn't it?

But however brilliant that campaign might be, we can go further with marketing UK Plc. How about "Britain is Getting Greater"? Or "Britain is Great Again"? "Up a Creek but we've got a Paddle – and it's Made in Britain"? Or, particularly for our former colonies, "Empire II – Return of the British"?

Brexit itself will be rebranded as "The Great Escape", complete with that catchy tune and imagery of prison camps: that's the kind of British humour that plays surprisingly well on the continent. (Just ask Boris!) And given how Brexit will resemble England's ongoing travails on the soccer pitch, maybe we could ensure that every Brexit-related event – speech, rally, trade fair – has a talentless band playing the theme from *The Great Escape* in the background, really badly, over and over again, until you think you're going mad.

This is good...

And for the export markets, some really eye-catching themes. Edgy was the word the creatives kept using – appropriate, given that's where Britain now is – and the same people who brought you the FCUK campaign to sell some cheap and nasty clothes will be doing the same for UK Plc. Out will go the dowdy old Made in Britain label. In comes:

Britain - it's fUKing brilliant!

This will be seen on everything from pots of jam to bottles of whisky, JCB diggers to packets of aspirin.

It's nothing short of a corporate identity for Brexit!

But this is... dare one say it... brilliant! .

Property

Britain is an island, thank God. No land borders with those ghastly Europeans. (If you don't believe me, take a walk in any direction and you'll eventually reach the sea, but still be surrounded by warm beer, red post-boxes, Ford Transits and litter, so proving you are still in Britain.) As an island, Britain has always had a limited supply of land. And the Law of Supply and Demand means that British land is always a great long-term bet for making money.

Now of course in business long-term bets are fine, but what we really want are short-term certainties. And the great thing about land is it can make you huge amounts of money in the short term, and be a safe long-term investment. It was this that led me to seek out Lord Arndale, as he later became, the doyen of the commercial property world, and offer him my services.

Lancelot Arndale, as he then was, had started with a million pounds and within a few short years had turned this into a fortune. His method was simple: buy up property on the cheap, and sell it at the top of the market. When he launched his career, most property was subject to rent control, which meant that once you were a tenant, the last thing you wanted was to do was to move, because as a tenant your rent was kept artificially low, but if you moved you'd have to pay the market rate for your new home. Better still, your tenancy couldn't be ended by the landlord. So long as you kept paying your pittance of a rent, you were safe. The only draw-back was that the landlord, who would be making very little on the property, was unlikely to invest in it (replacing windows, putting in central heating or inside toilets and so on) because they had no way to make a return on that investment.

Now that's the kind of challenge that inspires the British entrepreneur. Lord Arndale saw that, if you bought the freehold of properties with sitting tenants, and then persuaded those tenants to leave, the value of the property would immediate go up enormously. The persuasion could be contracted out to various colourful characters, who would ensure that the tenants soon felt it was time to move on. Installing prostitutes or drug dealers in the same building was one technique. Finding 'problem' tenants to drag down the neighbourhood another. And of course you could ensure that the tenants become increasingly (and literally) untenable by neglecting basic maintenance – which also improved the scanty profits you made from rents. Lord Arndale wasn't alone in this kind of dynamic asset management. And fortunately for his future career, the bleeding-heart types who objected to it ended up concentrating their ire on a minor player called Rachmann.

So when Lancelot began to move upmarket, into commercial property, he came with a clean sheet. And with a good amount of capital behind him, he could start to think big. The fashion at the time was for large-scale redevelopment of city centres, in part because of growing traffic meant the old Victorian or medieval street plans were getting clogged up. These were managed by local government planners and councillors, who were the key people that Arndale wanted to influence, so they would see their way to placing the task of redevelopment in his hands. Most of these were annoyingly stand-offish – even simple, friendly gestures such as dropping off a case of whisky at Christmas with the head of planning or offering a hard-working councillor a free holiday in the Balearics for him and his family would be misinterpreted as attempting to provide undue influence. But there were enough who would receive such tokens in the spirit with which they were offered to ensure that Arndale's office was soon awash with development opportunities.

The great thing about these big civic schemes was that all the small people – the independent shops and landlords – could be swept up into a single master-plan run by Arndale, using the compulsory purchase powers granted to local authorities. Sometimes there would be local protests about the prospect of a much-loved landmark such as a theatre or town hall having to make way for one of Arndale's developments. Such backward-looking sentimentality can pop up in the most unlikely places – as if cities such as Bradford, Manchester or Liverpool could have buildings worth preserving – but it rarely lasted long. It's amazing how flammable much-loved buildings can be. (Theatres in particular seem to burst into flames at the drop of a match – or do I mean hat? In fact, I still feel a bit nervous when attending performances of the shows penned by my old bobsleigh team-mate, Lloyd 'Lord' Webber, in case the building turns into an inferno during the second act.)

There is very little of my time at Arndale Securities that it seems sensible to share with you now. They were times where the buccaneering spirit was very much to the fore and there were some unfortunate headlines when one of our favourite associates, John Poulson, was convicted of corruption. Suffice it to say that, despite the boom and bust nature of the property market, it has all been one way over the long term. And the busts are as good as the booms, if you know the market better than other investors.

Look at the London property market. In times of boom, investors from around the world pile in, because it's seen as a safe haven. London property also has the advantage that, when you come to sell, your money comes out whiter than white, whatever colour it was when it went in. Property developers run up the kinds of flats that overseas investors like – views but no gardens is the preference, although as the new owners usually never set foot in the flat (indeed, many of them cannot set foot in Britain because of outstanding Interpol warrants) it doesn't really matter what they are like.

As with any bubble, it will burst. The trick in property is to see the crash coming – and that's a lot easier when you are in the business, rather than a speculative investor in Singapore or St Petersburg – and stop building. You turn everything into cash, wait for the market to bomb (which converting to cash will help accelerate) and then allow the dust to settle, at which point you can use that cash to buy up the wreckage and start the market heading upwards once more.

This can all sound a bit selfish. You might ask where the social contribution comes from. But actually, the property cycle is hugely patriotic, if you look at it in the right way. Say I'm Lord Arndale. I sell a flat to John Foreigner for £1 million. Then there is a property crash. Mr Foreigner wants to sell (perhaps because of liquidity issues or a pending court case for corruption, treason or bestiality in his home country) so I buy it back for £500,000. Then the property bubble starts inflating again, and I sell the flat to Mr Oligarch for £2 million. I, on behalf of Britain Plc, have brought in foreign earnings of £1.5 million. And if I do this across my entire property portfolio of thousands of flats, you soon get into the billions. How many of Britain's industrial sectors can boast that kind of foreign currency earning potential?

And if you are working hard to bring in much-

London property: our most profitable export.

needed dollars, roubles and euros for the British economy, then of course there's no point sitting on them. It's important to spend that money on French impressionists, Italian supercars and Caribbean islands (not spending the money *in* the islands, but actually buying them). This does slightly reduce the benefit to Britain's balance of payments – but you show me the British islands that have the right climate and a local workforce with key skills such as shark-fishing, limbo dancing and mixing planter's punch.

I had some very good times with Lord Arndale. And now I have a decent pot to invest in UK property, ready to tank as Brexit sets in, those good days will soon roll again.

Agriculture

One of the ways in which the EU managed to discredit itself with the British public was the subsidies it paid to famers. For years the Common Agricultural Policy generated awful headlines for Brussels, from wine lakes and butter mountains to tales of Corsican inventing millions of goats to benefit from Transitional Upland Goat Relief, or German agri-criminals cheerfully passing off horse meat as Bulgarian bratwurst.

So one of the few certainties about the next few years is that farmers are going to have it bad. Real bad. No more subsidies, grants, payments, transitional arrangements, price support or market interventions. Even if we wanted to go on featherbedding Britain's farming industry, we couldn't. It's not just the rules of the World Trade Organisation that prevent it. It's also that, when we start negotiating all these amazing trade deals with Canada, New Zealand, Barbados and the rest, the first thing on their list will be opening up our markets to Canadian wheat, New Zealand lamb and Barbadian sugar. Which will mean, I'm sorry to say, shafting British wheat, sheep and sugar-beet farmers. At least they'll have the satisfaction, as they hand back the keys to the combine harvester and watch the family farms go under the auctioneer's hammer, that it's in the National Interest.

Indeed, one of the unexpected pleasures that will come from Brexit will be to watch the faces of all those lefties who think that the EU vote was a cry of anguish about globalisation, and how Brexit was a chance to turn back the clock. In fact, we're going to be more globalised than ever. More competition from overseas, and less chance to impose standards on the environment, public health or workers' conditions. I've wagered a case of Chateau Mouton Rothschild '68 with one of the chaps at the Claremount Club that the first of them to crack mentally will be Larry Elliott, the *Guardian's* economics editor, and that by 2021 he'll be in an asylum for the criminally naive.

Anyway, don't be disheartened by all this. Losing a few farmers is actually a good thing, as they currently take up land that could be used for hunting, shooting or housing. Above all, we need more country estates. The idea of owning 5,000 acres and setting up as a country gent is what drives many business people towards their first £100 million and we need to keep this as an affordable dream.

So the future of British agriculture is clear. A few estates for the Wealth Creators. A few organic farms to keep the Waitrose classes happy. And few massive agri-factories producing cheap broiler chickens to feed the masses. Which jut shows that, with Brexit, there's something for everyone.

PART THREE:

OUR GREAT NEW BRITISH ECONOMIC MIRACLE

The New Economy

When I took on the role of Chairman of Brexit Solutions, one of the first things I did was to break the rule of a lifetime and talk to an expert. After all, I didn't want to be caught out recommending something that went against my own sense of what was right for Britain. So I had dinner with one of those academic-wallahs at Cambridge, calculating that even if his advice were duff, I'd get some decent port out of it. Professor Lee was the name I was recommended. As it turned out, he was a she. (I remember some nonsense about women priests a few years back, but when did they allow women to become academics?) Even more startling, she was young and, for a brainy girl, rather attractive.

I listened indulgently as she explained that she was writing a paper on what she called the Farage Paradox for some obscure journal or other. Then she went into a long explanation about how Britain's economic success depended on migrants, who in turn were attracted to Britain by its economic success. A 'virtual spiral of cumulative causation' was her phrase for it. (I know because I got her to write it down, and suggested she might just add her phone number afterwards.)

'And is that what Brexit will bring?' I asked.

'No,' she replied, her deep brown eyes widening in surprise, and a hint of a smile playing on those cherry-red lips. 'The corollary of the upwards spiral is a downwards spiral. Limiting economic migration will harm the economy, so making the UK less attractive for migrants and for investment.'

'My dear girl, is there any evidence for that?'

'You could cite the fact that the world economies with the lowest levels of inwards economic migration and investment are those with the worst economic performance, such as Yemen and North Korea.'

'And what has that to do with Nigel?'

'It's because he wants a prosperous Britain with limited migration.'

I found all this rather hard to follow – the port really was bloody good, and the little curl of hair behind her ear kept distracting me – but fortunately she wrote it down as well. And here it is.

I've kept this as a memento of a most pleasant evening and a touchstone for Brexit planning. As Little Miss May keeps saying, Brexit means Brexit, by which she means 'if we don't get rid of the foreigners, we're political toast.' And when Nigel and the others interpret the 'will of the people' it is always in terms of 'getting back control of our borders'. The post-referendum 'choice' was whether Brexit meant staying in the Single Market and minimising the economic impact, or leaving the Single Market and maximising the potential to kick out Johnnie European. Obviously we want to be prosperous. But at least if we can't have prosperity, it will scare off the bloody migrants, so delivering what the British people wanted more than anything.

And that is the beauty of Farage's Paradox. Brexit will not only allow us to keep out foreigners. It will, by trashing the economy, stop foreigners wanting to come here in the first place.

The Farage Paradox

1. Since joining the EU, Britain's economy has become more and more successful.

2. That success has brought in more and more workers from abroad.

3. A lot of people in Britain don't like all these foreigners coming here.

4. The only way to reflect the democratic will of the British people is to fuck up the economy, so foreigners won't want to come here any more.

5. Leaving the EU is the fastest and most certain way to fuck up the economy.

Wealth Creation

One of the things I learned working for Tiny Rowland was that there's no relation between the wealth of a country and the wealth of the people running it. You'd fly in to a dirt-poor country like Zambia and there'd be plenty of Johnnie Walker in the shops, tinted-windowed Mercedes on the roads, and dollars on the casino tables, whatever else was going on in the slums outside. In fact, one such trip to seal the deal on a tobacco plantation in Zaire, where you could hardly have eaten better or drunk finer wines in Paris itself (and believe me, I've tried), led me to coin Futtock's Ninth Law:

"The poorer the country, the richer the rulers."

The election of my old blackjack partner Don Trump hasn't changed this rule. For one thing, he's probably worth less than a billion dollars, and that would put him in the middle rank of African despots. Maybe a few years at the helm of the world's largest economy will see his net worth, and that of his extended family, friends and associates, tick up a point or two. After all, when he promised to Make America Great Again, I don't think he had a Lynden Johnson-style Great Society or a Roosevelt New Deal in mind, but something a bit more Reaganite and trickle-down, and where better to start things trickling than with your nearest and dearest? But even if a Trumpian economic miracle were to boost America's wealth creators, it won't change the fundamentals. Wealth isn't just about the amount of cash you have, the length of your yacht or the square footage of Impressionist paintings on your walls. It's about power.

If you have money, you can do what you like. When my old mate Alan Clarke was Minister for Trade, with a rather nice room at the top of a plush office block, he used to look out of the window and wonder what would happen if he urinated down on the little people making their dull little ways up and down Victoria Street. Do you think he could have even thought of such a thing, let alone do it (and I like to think he *did* do it, though his diaries are silent on that question) had he not had a castle in Kent to fall back on? The thing about having loads of boodle is it makes you independent – fearless, ready to stick to your principles, unbowed by any petty considerations, because if it comes to it, you can walk out and not worry about your next pay check or who has control of your pension.

Money is also the ultimate defence. It can buy you security, armed guards, the best lawyers, allow you to bribe the lawmakers or pay for you to live a pleasant life on the run. Look at Marc Rich. His contact-book was a who's who of the world most evil and blood-stained rulers, from Ayatollah Khomeini to General Pinochet, but he was also feted in his adopted homeland for his philanthropic works. His companies were indicted on countless criminal charges, but his own legal woes – on the FBI's most wanted list for a decade – ended when President Clinton gave him a pardon. ('Gave' may not be quite the right word: the fact that Rich's ex-wife had given nearly half a million dollars to the Clinton Library amongst other Clinton-related gifts did lead to a few raised eyebrows.) And even when holed up in Switzerland, Rich didn't do too badly.

Money means you can insulate yourself from most of life's unpleasantnesses. It also means you can do what you want in a more positive way – whether its surrounding yourself with beautiful things, doing good works, funding extremist political movements or simply indulging in long-term vendettas. My old Cleudo partner Jimmy Goldsmith, for example, did all four. If he wanted to send a video to millions of British voters promoting his cranky Referendum Party, he simply got out his cheque-book and the thing was done. Just as he could bid for the finest paintings at auction, or spend decades trying to close down *Private Eye*. Most of all, he enjoyed it all immensely. I miss him still.

In a democracy, there are a few small limits on what you can do, even if you are insanely rich. Take Lord Lucan. He murdered his nanny and attempted to do the same for his wife. Naturally, his chums rallied round. Of course, one couldn't sweep the whole thing under the carpet. This isn't some tin-pit banana republic. Instead, we all chipped in, got him out of the country, new identity and so on. Which shows that suggestions that it's one law for the rich in Britain and one law for the rest of you is bunkum. Any group of east-end gangsters would have done the same for one of theirs. (When I visited John in the Tibetan monastery where he spent his latter years, far from the gaming tables of Whites and with little prospect of ever sitting behind the wheel of his beloved Aston Martin once more, I didn't think to myself: 'here is one of Britain's privileged classes'. I saw a man who, by entertaining the nation with thirty years of speculation, and by distracting a number of senior police officers from investigating other matters such as tax evasion amongst the business elite, had paid his debt to society.)

But the benefits of living in a democracy outweigh any such minor inconveniences. First, dictatorships are prone to change. I don't here mean minor changes, such as the substitution of a bunch of low-rent, venal, incompetent, self-serving and sexually-deviant Tory politicians for a bunch of low-rent, venal, incompetent, self-serving and corrupt Labour ones. I mean the kind of change where members of the elite have to make an unseemly dash to the airport, leaving behind valuable personal possessions such as paintings, vintage cars and mistresses. Modern democracy, buttressed by a vibrant media which is owned by the right kind of people, and a vibrant political scene in which the right kind of people can make an influential contribution to national life, gives the wealth creators the best of both worlds: stability, and the opportunity to enjoy our wealth without too many restrictions or inconvenient questions.

Money also gives you status. It provides an entrée into worlds that would otherwise remain closed, where you can mingle with the most interesting and glamorous people, the movers and shakers, the glitterati: people like Noel Edmonds, the Spice Girls and that chap who runs Sports Direct who looks like a toad. Money also buys you pots of influence. Dear Peter Mandelson could never resist an invitation to join me on my yacht off Antibes, where he could be guaranteed to meet luminaries such as ITV's Dickie Davies, David "the Hoff" Hasellhoff and Nadia Tsainidova, once the Kirov's leading star and now Vladimir Putin's personal chemist. Heady stuff for the son of a tin miner from Penwith.

So the gaining of money is a means to an end. Power, influence, protection. And this goes to the heart of Brexit.

Human nature means that we care most for those closest to us, and less for those further away. We care most of all for ourselves, and then – like the layers of an onion – we care for our family, our friends, our dogs and racehorses, our business colleagues, acquaintances and current and former mistresses, and so on through the communities around our various residences, the countries they are in, and finally the rest of the world. What this means in practice is that we ought to be free to help those nearest to us. Take Cassiope, the daughter of one of my oldest friends, who is currently looking to join a merchant bank. And what a sensible choice, given the social life, the international travel and the money. But jobs in merchant banking are much in demand, and you need to have a foot on the ladder, and what better way to do that than to take up an internship at another merchant bank where you can gain experience, meet all the right people, and generally show you'll fit in.

But there's a movement afoot to put a stop to this. It's seen as elitist. The argument goes that young people who don't have uncles, aunts or godparents who have such opportunities in their gift are in some way put at a disadvantage by the way in which plum internships are awarded without an open competition. The usual claptrap about disadvantage and privilege is wheeled out. As a sensible person, you can see the flaws in that argument. For example, if my own children, Horatio, Belleraphon and Minxie, had wanted to join the fire brigade, or go down a coal mine, they would have run into exactly the same kinds of barriers as a slum child from Barnsley might in relation to merchant banking, the law or joining the BBC. As everyone knows, jobs in the fire brigade are handed down from generation to generation, and no doubt the same would be true in coal mining, if there were any pits still left open. And it also shows how this is simply human nature – and that any attempts to control it are essentially and deeply unnatural, in the same way that other things are deeply unnatural, such as goat porn or eating marmalade in a sandwich.

And where do such threats come from? Not directly from the European Commission. The threat is more insidious. Rather there is a hidden nexus between the Commission and other Euro-conspirators and the Liberal Elite in their north London ghettos. Some uppity prole complains that her little Tyson or Barbarella didn't get an internship in international banking just because they didn't go to the right school or know the right people. This is reported on the BBC. Polly Toynbee writes a whinge-a-thon in *The Guardian*. A north London lawyer offers to take her case to the European Court for free, perhaps on behalf of that ghastly pop merchant Bono. And before you know it, the Liberal-Intelligensia-Euro-Elite have banned us from caring for those close to us in the traditional way.

(In passing, it's one of Europe's better-kept secrets that the European Court keeps moving between Strasbourg and Luxembourg. Every week, I expect. When I tried to find out how much this legal cavalcade costs the hard-pressed taxpayer, the spokeswoman for the court simply laughed, then put the phone down on me. Rather an attractive laugh, though. I may try again.)

What we now face in Britain is an existential conflict between a new liberal, Europhile, metrosexual elite and the old, traditional, stalwart British conservative elite. Since the 1960s, the liberals have been gaining ground, with their legalisation of homosexuality, their equal rights for women and black people and their male grooming products. It's time we turned the clock back, with people taking up their natural roles once more and a return to the smell of damp tweed, sandlewood aftershave and sweat in Britain's public places. Out with the tofu, infusions and reiki that have infiltrated our national life, and in with anchovy paste, cocoa, and Swedish masseusses.

(As an illustration of how bad things have become, have you noticed how, in Britain today, it's sometimes hard to become unreasonably angry about things, because they are simply incomprehensible? Take quinoa. It's clearly a bad thing and entirely un-British – but what is it? A kind of yoga? Venezuelan goat's cheese? You see the problem.)

This is a battle where we have to choose sides.

I have chosen the side that will win: that is, the side of the reactionaries. Why? Not because I myself am a reactionary. Nor, on a personal level, do I actively dislike liberals. But at the end of the day, in the kind of social breakdown and civil conflict that will follow Brexit, the conservatives are going to win. We have the newspapers on our side. We have the money. We have, when all is said and done, the police and the Army. And a bunch of chanting trots, George Monbiot and some people in Guy Fawkes masks blowing whistles is not going to win the day.

What form will this clash take? How will we win? What should be our battle cry?

Some people might say we need to Make Britain Great Again. Of course, that's true. But the priority is to Make Britain British Again.

Brexit is our chance to do that. It's a victory to the forces of 1953 and a slap in the face for self-appointed progressives of every hue. By pulling out of Europe, we can begin the process of National Purification. And the first place we'll start will be with Regulation.

Regulation

There's that glorious moment when you come to the edge of a town and village, in your vintage sports coupé, doing no more than 50-55 mph, and you pass those 'derestricted' road signs and at last you can really let the Old Girl go. There's no feeling like it. It's joys like this that make life worth living. But in the European Province of Britannia, such joys are harder and harder to experience.

It's much the same in business. Business is at its most enjoyable when you wake up one day and think... I know, let's buy Harrods, close the bloody thing down, and sell it off for flats for a quick profit. Or... You wouldn't believe how much oil there is under Stonehenge. Let's get the rigs in and drill us a well. Or... well, all the things that would turn an honest penny but which, more than anything else, would be fun. A dawn raid on a competitor's shares. Putting a chemicals firm into liquidation to avoid the clean-up costs. Sacking the workforce and reemploying them the next day on zero-hours contracts. What's the point of being at the top of a firm, with all the power, unless you're allowed to use it?

That's what makes we business people hate regulation so viscerally. It's not that the rules are themselves always bad. It's that they are rules, telling us what we can and can't do. I might want to give my staff a pension, but I don't want some talentless, camera-hunting politician to make me do it. I might want to avoid polluting a river – particularly if one of my chums has the fishing rights further downstream – but damned if some jobsworth government inspector should come round and check up on me. Regulation doesn't just add to a business's costs, or prevent it from competing with the rest of the world. It also cuts down on our chances, as captains of industry, to do the right thing.

It's not just Europe that creates bureaucracy. It goes right back to the Victorians with their legislation on chimney sweeps and the slave trade and other examples of interference in the rights of businesses to go about their business.

The key is, only businessmen can also see the Big Picture. If you insist on expensive equipment to remove the very remote risk of a chemicals factory polluting a local river, then that means the company will make less profit and so pay less in Corporation Tax. That could mean less for defence spending, leading to an invasion by Russia or Afghanistan or whoever. Or less for the National Health Service, resulting in the deaths of angelic little children. Or the firm might have to sack half its workers, leading to unemployment, crime, suicides and perhaps even, in some of our more deprived regions, cannibalism.

Take the dead hand of Britain's health and safety culture. In the buccaneering, risk-taking Brexit world, we need leaders ready to put their businesses on the line to chase higher profits, like George Simpson at Marconi. We are not going to foster the next generation of leaders if we wrap our young people up in cotton wool, or if we create a society in which every little risk has to be assessed and labelled. We need speed-merchants, thrill-seekers and devil-may-care types at the helms of our major corporations – people not afraid to interpret financial regulations or environmental controls in imaginative ways.

Some risks we can export to other countries. So with manufacturing, one of the advantages of making things in China or Burma (or ideally in countries you've never even heard of) is that when – as inevitably happens from time to time – the factories explode in fireballs of death, or turn the local environment into a toxic hell, then it need not disturb the economic life of Britain. We simply find another community on the far side of the world willing to be part of our economic partnership, on a dollar a day, with armed guards on the doors and suicide nets over the stairwells thrown in for free.

And you can even put some risks entirely outside international jurisdiction. We do this already with shipping. Register your boat in Britain, and there are all kinds of tedious inspection regimes and crewing standards to follow. But register it with Liberia or the North Sandwich Islands and you find you have a much lighter-touch regime, leading to lower costs and a more competitive business. Some of these 'flags of convenience' (so well-named, as they mean you can flush your intrusive British maritime standards down the toilet) essentially allow ship-owners to do as they see fit, which is just as it should be. Ship-owners understand shipping better than these so-called experts, and we have every interest in ensuring that the cargo arrives safely at its destination (except if we are engaged in maritime fraud, where the loss of a ship can be a profitable outcome, particularly if the cargo was insured too, but somehow never actually ended up on board the ship – but rest assured that this is a very small segment of the overall market).

And businesses are rising to the challenge. I am involved in a new venture that is exploring the possibilities of bringing offshore manufacturing operations closer to the UK. This would mean buying up redundant oil platforms from the North Sea and converting them into factories to manufacture pesticides, fireworks, asbestos products, genetically-modified organisms and other processes currently struggling under the over-protective regime of the European Union. These could then be moored conveniently just outside the UK's territorial waters,

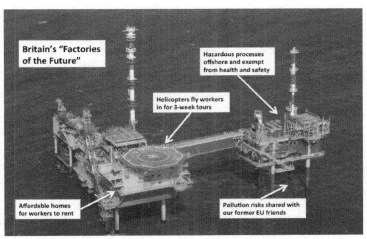

The future of British manufacturing: Clean, Green and a very long way from Surrey.

© Department for Industry

where no kinds of regulations at would apply – just like in the Far East. Then British workers could be flown out by helicopter, for a month or so at a time, to carry out the actual manufacturing – so giving a welcome boost to local employment. Over time, we could develop entire offshore industrial estates conveniently placed for areas of maximum unemployment such as Newcastle and Lowestoft. Perhaps this could be extended to call centres, using life-expired cruise ships. The possibilities are so exciting.

The essential message here is that businesses are the ones best placed to make these difficult judgments about the balance between your risk and our reward.

And fortunately, those blasted EU regulations will soon be a thing of the past.

One of the hidden opportunities of Brexit is the rather tedious-sounding section 2(1) of the European Community Act 1972 which Camilla dug out for me.

2(1) All such rights, powers, liabilities, obligations and restrictions from time to time created or arising by or under the Treaties, and all such remedies and procedures from time to time provided for by or under the Treaties, as in accordance with the Treaties are without further enactment to be given legal effect or used in the United Kingdom shall be recognised and available in law, and be enforced, allowed and followed accordingly; and the expression and similar expressions shall be read as referring to one to which this subsection applies.

It is this one short piece of legislation that turns Euro-law into British law. In other words, all the thousands of EU Regulations and Directives on everything from bankers' bonuses to protecting birds only have legal effect because of those few words.

And that makes the prospect of abolishing Section 2(1) rather tasty.

Little Miss May has proposed a replacement for Section 2(1) so that all the existing euro-law will be converted directly into British law. Very wise of her. After all, we don't want anyone to be worried about this while there's still some faint chance of reversing the decision to leave the EU. But once Brexit is irreversible, and Parliament comes to actually repeal the 1972 Act, then we can nuance that position. Instead of simply accepting everything that Europe has dreamed up over the last 44 years, we can dump the lot all at once.

No more controls on paying bankers proper bonuses or building on bird sanctuaries. No more restrictions on how long we can make our employees work, or rights to have time off for maternity or, God help us, paternity.

Instead, we can go through the catalogue of Euro-legislation and decide what we want to keep.

If anything.

For once you turn the thing upside down, and see that we don't actually have to have any of this legislation at all, then it becomes amazingly liberating. You flick through all these Directives and think, do I really need any of this at all. It's like one of those reality TV programmes that people like you watch, where a pair of perky presenters go into the overstuffed house of a congenital hoarder and advise them of how to dispose of their collections of dusty teapots or old, fading copies of *Home Studio Recording*. And the advice? Just chuck the lot!

Imagine the sense of release as these all go in the bin: Directive 2009/148/EC on exposure to asbestos at work; Directive 92/91/EEC on mineral-extracting industries (drilling); Directive 2011/83/EU on consumer rights; Directive 2004/49/EC on safety on the Community's railways; Directive 2009/127/EC amending Directive 2006/42/EC with regard to machinery for pesticide application.

And these are just an appetiser. There are some big ones to get rid of. Directives on Environmental Impact Assessment, Working Time, Financial services, Distance selling. On and on.

It's time Britain's whaling stations, like this one on South Georgia, were back in action supplying the lucrative Japanese market. Once we are free of EU Regulation 337/97 on the trade in wildlife, then it's Thar She Blows!

Now you might think – Reg, are you perhaps biting off more than you can chew. After all, every interest group in Britain from the unions to the Women's Institute is going to try and protect some or other of this legislation.

And of course, you have a point. But you must look forward to the kind of world we will be in by that time. Britain will be cutting ties with its largest market. Jobs will be flowing from London to Dublin, Paris and Luxembourg. Japan, the US and China will be diverting their inward investment to the Netherlands and Poland. Companies like HSBC and GSK will be relocating to the continent.

In the face of this looming catastrophe, our rhetoric that Britain must become more competitive to survive in the post-Brexit world will have considerably more power. It will a new Project Fear – the fear that, if we retain any kind of protection for consumers, employees or the environment, we will be consigning ourselves to a future rather reminiscent of Cambodia under Pol Pot, only with worse weather. That will make people see sense.

Employment

It was while I was at British Leyland that a chance encounter on the shop floor at the Preston plant changed my life. I was chatting to one of the shop stewards, and although I could only understand about one word in five – I never got used to those thick Brummie accents – I worked out he was talking about something called economic rent. Well, that caught my attention because that was way above the pay grade for these salt-of-the-earth mechanical types. So I asked him to tell me more, and before I knew it he had pressed a well-thumbed paperback in my hands. It was entitled Marx on Economics, but it wasn't by the Russian revolutionary who gave the world Marxism, Communism, Stalin and all that. It was by a German economist called Karl Marx and it was an absolute revelation.

Karl's central thesis was that wealth creation depends on labour and capital. Labour is people doing the work. Capital means land, buildings, machinery, raw materials and the cash to fund business activity, including research and development, advertising, and appropriate incentives for senior management. And both need to be rewarded – through wages for labour, and through dividends on shareholdings or interest on loans for capital (and as banks are funded by shareholders, it all comes back to them in the end). Broadly speaking, if wages go up, then there's less money left for the shareholders; and if you reward the shareholders by increasing dividends, then that means squeezing wages.

And that has to be a balance. If the employees start jumping up and down saying they want more money, is has to come from somewhere, doesn't it? And that somewhere will be the hard-pressed shareholder who has lent his money to help the business get going and who naturally wants a bit back in return.

This is where Karl and I part company. Karl thought that paying people just because they had accumulated capital over the years was a bad thing, because it created injustices in society. I believe you have to give a good deal to shareholders, otherwise there's the risk that society becomes too equal. And what's the point of striving to get to the top if you're not that much better off when you get there?

Now you might say, wait a minute Reg, if we pay our workers more, then there'll be more money in the economy, and this will create more demand for goods and services, and so make more money for businesses, won't there? But I would say to you, you old Keynesian dinosaur, that this ignores the crucial fact that workers and shareholders are not the same kind of people.

By definition, workers have no real money. They have failed to set aside the kinds of capital that would allow them to invest in our economic future while still leaving enough for a yacht, BUPA, and a share in a racehorse or two. They have probably spent the money that they could have put into Investment Trusts or Impressionist Art on Stella Artois, payday loans and nappies for their excessive numbers of offspring.

I make no moral judgement about this. We live in a free country, and how people squander their chances in life is a matter for them. But I do contrast them with shareholders. The latter have real money. In other words, the system has rewarded them, and that in turn means they (or their parents) must be people of greater moral worth, who have contributed more to society, than mere workers. And it's quite right that the system should reward them in this way. As the Bible says, to those who have, more shall be given.

Anyway, back to Marx. The point I take from it is this. As a country, we want more people with capital, and fewer workers. Running businesses with workers is jolly difficult. I know. I've done it. And I've also seen the contrast with banking, insurance, finance, legal services and all these other businesses where you don't really have 'workers' in the traditional sense at all. It was this contrast that led me to coin Futtock's Ninth Law of Business:

> *"Managing money is a lot easier than managing people. And it pays better too."*

You'll remember my point about all those trouble-makers in the nineteenth century, asking for a say in how the country is run. Well, it's no surprise that the ring-leaders were all skilled artisans, not everyday grubby labourers. They had the confidence and intelligence to challenge the status quo. In the twentieth century, their descendants were the skilled workers at the heart of our major manufacturers, much given to political activity and striking for better wages and working conditions. I ask you, is it reasonable to ask an employer to give you a job when you're hell-bent on putting that employer out of a job himself, by nationalising his factory?

So it's no surprise that, over the second half of the twentieth century, we gradually got out of manufacturing. Industry by industry, the great names have gone. Swan Hunter, Cammell Laird and Austin and Pickering in shipbuilding. Norton and BSA in motorcycles. Dennis and Leyland in buses. Foden, Scammell, Leyland and ERF in trucks. Lansing in fork-lifts. Pye in televisions.

In many ways, losing all those industries has been the best thing possible for Britain's economy. Instead of having to train all these skilled workers in manufacturing – lathe operators and the like – we can concentrate on a few very well-paid jobs in finance and the professions.

Of course, we do still make things in Britain. But usually it's where foreigners take on the drudgery of industrial relations, as at Nissan and Toyota. Our own manufacturers generally survive where we are in an industrial sector that is safely protected from the cold winds of market forces, or where the actual manufacturing takes pace somewhere else.

My good friend Johnny Dyson, for example, makes all kinds of useful gadgets and has built up a very successful business on the back of it. Hats off to him, I say. But while he has lots of well-paid designers and marketing people in Britain, the stuff itself is made in the Far East. Perfect. We get some well-paid middle-class jobs for the kind of people who would never dream of going on strike or rocking the national boat, and the Malaysians or Chinese or whoever can get on with the dreary task of making the stuff, helped by having a no-nonsense attitude to industrial relations.

This is what makes new technology so exciting. Computers mean you can employ people and never even have to meet them. If I want to run a taxi firm, I can ensure that I never have to come face to face with my drivers. In fact, by only using owner-drivers, I can pretend that they are not employees at all, but sub-contractors – or even better, that I am not providing the service to my customers, but instead enabling those customers to find a taxi, and providing some administrative services to go with it (such as booking the cab, taking the money, ensuring that the driver probably isn't a rapist, and so on). Brilliant, isn't it? I can set up a huge, vastly profitable international business and all I need are some computer geeks and a lot of lawyers.

The only disappointment is that most of these firms have been started up in the US. Once, Britain led the way in exploiting workers. Now, it's the Yanks doing it on a massive scale, while all we have is some old-fashioned maltreatment of fruit-pickers in the wilds of Lincolnshire. Where's the vision? The ambition?

We are moving into a post-employment world, and I want Britain to be leading the pack. Take retail. My old golfing chum Michael Ashley has done some great work at Sports Direct. Making your staff go through a lengthy search after they've clocked off – so you are no longer paying them while it happens – is just the kind of innovation this country needs if we are to remain competitive in the vital business of selling people overpriced trainers. But we must go further.

Why, for example, do we pay shop workers who are not serving staff? Surely it is only right that their remuneration should be related to the amount of customer experience they deliver? I'm a director of a very exciting tech start-up looking into exactly this opportunity. By using surveillance cameras and some clever software, we can monitor the exact moment when the customer comes up to the counter, and when they walk away with their purchase, and reward the staff member for the time the transaction takes, down to the last second. Not only does this keep down costs: it also incentives the lazy swine to stop checking their make-up or their InstaFace account and actually do some serving.

And why should we not have self-employed associates instead of employees in our offices, shops, bars and warehouses? We can track their every move, and this can be fed directly into an advanced billing system to generate invoices from their individual service companies that we would settle in the usual way (90 days if you're lucky). It isn't just about avoiding National Insurance or employment legislation (though that does help). Think of the healthy dose of competition it would bring to the workplace, where a simple move like helping a colleague clear the dirty dishes from a restaurant table would be the equivalent of winning market share. We'd be creating literally millions of new micro-businesses – some of which would go on to become the Wetherspoons and Byron Burgers of the future.

Now clearly, none of this is going to happen if we stay in the European Union. The UK would be dragged in front of the European Court of Justice and the other Member States would bleat on about undermining the social partnership between employers and workers. And that just shows how deep the rot has gone. I don't mind pretending that we want to get along with our staff. Under New Labour, for example, I was happy to talk about 'stakeholders' and 'social partners' along with the rest of them. But once people actually believe this stuff, there's no going back.

No, mark my words – if we want jobs (or rather, self-employment) in the future, we as employers and as a country need a free hand.

Immigration

During the referendum, the Leave campaign put a huge amount of work into linking Europe and immigration in people's minds. In reality, Europe was always pretty marginal to the British debate about immigration. Apart from some whining about Polish plumbers and Lithuanian sprout-pickers, no-one in Britain really gives a toss about European immigration. The xenophobes were against Arabs, Muslims, Africans, and Arab or African Muslims coming to Britain. And leaving the EU will make sod all difference to that.

So claiming Turkey was about to join the EU was perfect. It was utter bollocks, of course, but the great thing is that even when the Remainers were trying to tell people that, all the masses heard was 'Turkey... Europe... Millions of Muslims... Coming your way.' The phrase 'this story is a crock of horseshit' just didn't cut

I really don't see how anyone can think this is racist.

through the media debate.

This means that immigration is the litmus paper for Brexit. The British people have been promised that, on the day we leave the EU, we will Get Our Borders Back and the streets of London, Birmingham and Bradford will look like they did ethnically in the 1930s (or like Henley on Thames does today). And woe betide any politician who disappoints them.

But without immigration, Britain can't function. I won't rehearse the over-hyped and discredited alarmist propaganda of the Leave campaign, about the number of EU doctors and nurses in the UK, or the contribution EU workers make in the City of London; I'll just accept it's all true. So what do we do?

Little Miss May's approach is to make being a European in Britain less pleasant. Not stop them coming here at all, but just let them know that we don't really like them very much. So lots of filling in endless forms and intrusive questionnaires and visa application procedures, all of which will have a hefty fee attached to them. And we'll have lots of snide immigration officers saying 'Oh, really, Madam? And where exactly is this, ahem, café where you say you will be working?' and 'Could you just step over here, sir, out of the way of the British people waiting to come in?' That way, fewer Europeans will come here, so she'll score that way. But she can reassure employers that there are no actual bans on Europeans, so they can continue to use migration to fill the skills gaps left by our world-beating education system.

But will this be enough? The thing about revolutions is that they have a momentum of their own. People want stuff. We tell them they're going to get it. And before you know it, the ungrateful buggers are asking for more. It's never enough. That's all fine and dandy when it's consumerism, and we can sell them things to feed their endless greed. But when it comes to politics, it's much more tricky.

Luckily K. Calvin Kilman III, one of the leading men in the Leave campaign on all of this immigration stuff, turned down the chance to work on the Trump campaign to be head of thinking for Brexit Solutions instead. His anaylsis goes something like this.

Britain's economy needs migrants. But the British people don't want to live alongside them. So the logical answer is for British people and foreigners to live apart. That way, there'll be less tension, and we'll all be happier.

Also, the British people don't want to change their way of life, and they want any foreigners coming here to behave themselves according to the rules of this place. Like guests, you may say. Guest workers.

Britain isn't the only country to have faced this dilemma. Calvin's analysis reminds me forcefully of my time with the Anglo-Saxon Corporation in South Africa. There, the concern had been about bringing guest workers into areas mainly settled by whites. So we built accommodation for the men near the mines, but their families stayed in specially-designated 'homelands' some distance away, and that was where they voted as well.

It was the same in the big cities. Places like Jo'burg couldn't function without black workers to clean streets, offices and shoes; but they were not allowed to live in the city. Instead, townships were created as satellites outside the city boundaries, and some cheap and cheerful transport laid on – trains or minibuses – to get them to and from their place of work. All in all, it was a success.

Calvin's proposal is that we designate certain areas as Special Residential Districts, where European guest workers would be welcome. From there, special trains would take them to and from the centres of commerce. These districts would be self-sufficient, with their own schools, hospitals and police (locally-recruited, but with British officers). These places wouldn't be any kind of ghetto. British people would be allowed to live there, and no doubt some of the latte-sipping, bleeding-heart remainer-loving residents of Shoreditch or Crouch End would be only too eager to move there to take advantage of all the benefits of multiculturalism. For the rest of us, we could get on with being British.

We've tentatively identified four such SRDs:

• Bressex, to the east of London, taking in the less attractive parts of Essex (Thurrock and so on) but not places like Thaxted or Saffron Walden. This would service places such as Stansted and Felixstowe as well as London.

• Brexfolk in some of the flatter, muddier bits of Norfolk and Lincolnshire around King's Lynn and Sleaford, for all those sprout-pickers.

• Brexmoor, using some unproductive land with wonderful views (when it's not raining, anyway) to serve Bristol and the south-west agricultural sector.

• Brexitshire, based on some redundant army camps on Salisbury Plan, and providing a committed workforce for the Thames Valley and west London.

There would be system of permits and so on to ensure our guests stuck to the rules about where they went (there would be cafes, buses and so on outside the home lands reserved for their exclusive use) and we'd have to have some mechanisms to discourage our guests trying to marry their way into Britain proper. But these are all straightforward bureaucratic measures, and as well as the parallels I am familiar with from South Africa and Rhodesia, I understand

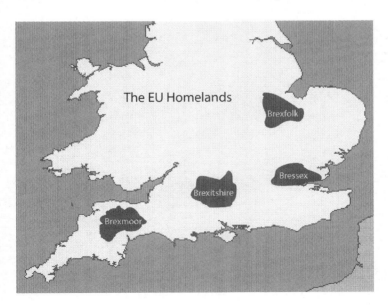

from Kevin that rather some similar rules in place in the southern United States until quite recently.

So, all in all, a most imaginative and forward-looking scheme. It may not feel, perhaps, at first sight, exactly *British* (although it reminds me of a time when all the immigrants lived in London's East End, and knew better than to start wandering around Mayfair or Kensington). But the thing about revolutions is that, if you want to stay in control, you have to keep ahead of curve. Just ask Trotsky!

Competition

Whatever else may be uncertain about Brexit Britain, one thing is clear. We're going to need to compete with the rest of the world to earn our living. No other country is going to give us a free lunch.

It shouldn't be that way, of course: having given the world computers, chemistry, television and the hovercraft, consumers around the world ought to be grateful to Britain and not run off and buy better and cheaper equivalents elsewhere.

But we are where we are: needing to compete. And we shouldn't be scared of taking on the best in the world and winning. We've done it before, as my time at British Airways shows.

It was John King, as he then was, who head-hunted me to come to BA. I'd been thinking of a move back to the UK anyway. South Africa was looking increasingly dicey. The Falklands in '82 had shown that Britain still had the backbone to fight a war to get it out of a political screw-up. And Margaret's subsequent victory at the 1983 general election meant that we'd have a business-friendly Prime Minister. It was she who'd appointed King to get British Airways, the loss-making state airline, ready to be sold off – in the newly-coined jargon, 'privatised' – and he wanted me to use my experience of strike-breaking in South Africa to help ram through the necessary changes.

King had a mammoth task on his hands. BA was inefficient, with an ageing fleet and a ramshackle network based more on the idea of 'flying the flag' as on making proper money. If the planes were old, the meals cold and the stewardesses more grumpy than a Bulgarian weight-lifter with a bad back, flying BA was still the patriotic thing to do. Fortunately, most other airlines were pretty dire too – Air France, TWA – but most of the time you couldn't fly with them anyway. Every route would have just two airlines on it: the chosen national 'champions' of the two countries at either end. So if you wanted to fly from London to Moscow, you could fly with a Soviet-style, command-economy, take-what-you're-given state airline, or you could fly Aeroflot. Choice, in effect, was like the choice between two forms of bowel disease. But at least it guaranteed profits from the captive flying customers, which paid for BA's bloated staffing and for it being forced to buy dud British planes.

John King had a simple plan to change this:

- Fire lots of staff
- Buy Boeing
- Employ the same fancy advertising agency who had helped Margaret win the election

He also saw that BA's main rivals were overseas: United and American Airlines. And for British Airways to compete with them, it needed a little less competition back home.

The first thing that Lord King said to me when I arrived at the BA head office was 'what the hell are you doing in my parking space?' But the second thing was to change my life: 'I believe profoundly in free enterprise, Reg. So I want you to get the government to crush all my rivals.'

British Airways had a brilliant track record in this department. In the 1970s, a buccaneering British businessman called Freddie Laker and his no-frills, low-cost airline had tried to expand to include routes across the Atlantic and down to Australia. BA was not having any of this, and for once our continental partners saw things the same way and joined BA in some predatory pricing. Laker went bust in 1982.

Since then, Air Europe and Dan-Air had gone the same way, and we'd bought out another rival, British Caledonian. No-one pointed the finger at BA (except for the owners, and the pilots and cabin crew who lost their jobs, but they were just a bunch of whingers – and anyway, with BA having 90% of the UK scheduled airline sector, if they wanted to work in the industry again, they knew to button their lips pronto).

The next challenger was a bit of a joke – a young chap with a beard, who knew nothing about aviation, and had just one plane. His gift for self-publicity couldn't be denied, but running an airline is a serious, grown-up business and I told John King that this Branson chap was clearly a flash in the pan.

At first, it seemed as if our tried-and-tested BA tactics would do the job. First, cut the fares on the routes where BA was in direct competition, and cross-subsidise them by keeping fares high on the others. Then 'bracket' each Virgin flight with a BA one timed to leave just before and another just after, so making the Virgin flight less attractive to customers and (because the route was flooded with excess seats) less profitable to Virgin. And finally, we'd up the standard of service on the competing routes by bringing in the most modern planes and even the most attractive cabin crew.

Unfortunately, it didn't work. While other rivals had competed on price, Virgin had pulled a fast one by competing on quality as well. And by going after business passengers, Virgin had made themselves less vulnerable to a price-war. Most of these business people weren't paying for the tickets themselves, and so were less impressed when BA cut its fares. They wanted a comfortable flight with high levels of service, and that's what BA struggled to deliver. Year after year, Virgin was voted best carrier on the Atlantic in the trade awards. All very embarrassing for me.

So we upped the competition by getting our PR types out there spreading a whole range of rumours about Virgin being unsafe or about to go bust. We also 'accessed' Virgin's computer data, which contained the contact details for all their passengers, and had a team of BA staff phoning them up and pretending to be from Virgin, to tell them that their flight was delayed but that they could book them on to BA at no extra cost. And we paid travel agents a cash bonus if they switched their customers from Virgin to BA.

This seemed like good, honest competition to me. But one or two weaklings within BA spilled the beans, the media started poking about, and before we knew it Branson had somehow turned the tables and got everyone talking about BA's 'dirty tricks'. It ended up in court, with BA making the biggest libel pay-out in British legal history. BA became one of the most hated brands in Britain, our customers swarmed to Virgin in droves, and that grinning pullover Richard Branson was splashed over every newspaper and TV channel in the world.

BA, though, is still much bigger than Virgin. Why? Because BA still has a monopolist grip on landing slots at Heathrow. Even if BA is no longer the world's favourite airline, it still pretty much controls the world's favourite airport, and what's good for BA is good for GB Plc. And that is why Futtock's Eighth Law of Business still holds true:

> *"The best way to hide a monopoly is to wrap it up in the Union Jack."*

So in Brexit Britain, there will be plenty of competition: us competing with the rest of the world. And if that means taking our foot off the competition pedal domestically, so be it. National champions are the future – firms like Vodafone, BT, BAe and Sky who can milk their British customers until their eyes water and use the cash to fund overseas adventures.

Yes, our post-Brexit economic miracle is going to be a truly national endeavour: because every man, woman and child in Britain is going to help pay for it through higher prices.

International Trade

If you want to win in world markets, you have to travel. That's what had led me to Mimi's, the finest brothel in Dusseldorf's famous Zugswangstrasse and one of the favourite haunts of Prince... well, let's call him Prince Colin, one of the less fragrant sprigs of that majestic and wide-spreading tree, the Saudi royal family. Colin was drinking Suze Spritzers, which was a new one to me, and neither the floor show nor the drink were quite to his taste. I didn't show it, but this left me a little concerned. Obviously the matter at hand, a significant arms order for my employers British Aerospace, was all about the product capabilities, price and financing, plus the aftercare that BAe could provide.

But there was also the before-care, as I like to think of it. I have always felt that my clients, and potential clients, need just as much looking after before they sign the deal as they do afterwards. They need to have their concerns soothed away. Concerns such as: what would become of me if there were a coup? Do I have enough cash in my Swiss bank account? Or how will I persuade Mitzi to do everything I want when I can't speak German? And you should know that your old friend Reg Futtock will see you right on all these counts.

I leaned forward.

'My dear Prince Hamza, perhaps when our business is concluded, I might have the honour to introduce you to another place of entertainment. It has...

shall we say, an unrivalled understanding of man of imagination.'

'Imagination?' Hamza replied, his face alight in the pulsing strobe lights of the club.

'Imagination beside which even the inventiveness of Sheherezade is mere grains of sand.' (There's a chap who got kicked out of the Foreign Office for reasons unspecified who used to teach us how to come out with this stuff.)

'Then why do we wait?' he asked, blowing out the sparkler on his drink.

'There is the matter of the tank contract...'

'Oh, I think your Scorpion is what the Royal Saudi armed forces need. Such a formidable name. And your most generous pre-financing package has convinced my colleagues that you are taking this matter more seriously than the French or the infidel Americans.'

We shook on it there and then, and I led him off to Club Z with the satisfaction of a job well done.

International trade isn't always as glamorous as that, of course. There's a lot of humdrum stuff like market research, developing dealer networks and so on. I tend to leave to those with a taste for that kind of thing. But for the Big Deals on which Britain's economic future now depends, there is nothing like the personal touch. You have to build up relations with the men with the money. You have to get inside their skin, understand their needs, their hopes and fears. You have to know their private bank account numbers and which of their offspring need what kind of help with their desire to travel to sun-kissed islands, buy crocodile handbags or service a spectacular drug problem. If they want to drink, you drink with them. If they want to fly to Paris and dine at *Le Tour d'Argent*, you make sure your company's private Dassault Falcon is on stand-by. If they want to go on about some dreary English soccer team, you make sure you can lay your hands on a shirt signed by their leading point-scorer. Take my word for it, this is hard work.

And we'll be doing a lot more of this post-Brexit. Fortunately, this is an area where we can compete with the best in the world. When it comes to pre-contract incentives and parallel finance channels, the Germans are too procedural and the Chinese too slow, the Russians can't be trusted and the Italians are wildly indiscreet. Occasionally the smaller nations pull off a coup – the Swedes, bless'em, are surprisingly good at bribery – but when push comes to shove, it's us, the Yanks and the French who lead the pack.

The Americans are very direct and of course they have plenty of cash. The French never really gave up on the idea of Empire, and have cleverly ensured that almost all of their 'former' colonies have a French-leaning strong man at the helm (and if any of them step out of line, there's always another Saint-Cyr trained Colonel ready to take their place, aided by some French paratroopers and a squadron of Mirages).

The British, though, got into this almost by accident. Or rather, by means of a few men of Vision. Chief amongst these was my old bivouac buddy and bridge partner David Stirling. He was an amazing chap, who had founded the SAS and taken part in any number of daring behind-enemy-lines raids. He was a natural for the Claremont Club. After all, it's a bit of an advantage in any game of chance when your opponent is distracted from their hand of cards by thinking how many men you've killed with your bare hands. (Seventy-nine was David's rough count, and he was not one for boasting.) But even high stakes at the casino table couldn't give David enough of a buzz in drab, post-War Britain. There was also a general theme amongst the Claremont Set that Britain was going down the drain – of which giving up on its Empire and getting in bed with the ghastly Europeans were the two worst signs. So they decided to do something about it.

Stirling happened to know the Saudi Prince Faisal, and sold him the idea of a mercenary army and air force. The Saudis had the money, but no experience in modern warfare. The British had the kit, the people, and the greed. Put it together, and you soon had British planes, tanks and the rest flowing into Saudi, and petro-dollars flowing back the other way.

The British government knew all about this, and encouraged it. In fact, once they realised just how much money you could make by selling arms, they couldn't get enough of it. And for once, the politicians could agree. The Tories liked it because it allowed them to play the Great Game again, meddling in the countries they were busily pulling down the Union Jack on. The Socialists liked it because of the jobs it brought. And they both liked it because of the money, and the chance to shift some dud kit made by the dud firms they were forced to prop up like BAC and Rolls.

Soon there was hardly enough red carpet in the country to welcome all the generals and dictators coming over here to stock up on anti-insurgency helicopters, snatch-squad Landrovers and 'interrogation equipment'. Yes, the bleeding heart liberals moaned on in the background, but we had the killer argument that if we didn't sell anti-personal mines or cattle-prods, someone else would. The French, probably.

Now you can't keep a money tree secret. Soon all kinds of strange people were crawling out to look for a feed. In Saudi, we had to wheel out bigger and bigger guns to help sell the guns. If the French sent President Mitterand, we'd send Mrs Thatcher. If the Americans invited King Faisal to the White House, he'd be booked in for a state dinner with the Queen followed by some parlour games at Windsor before the day was out. But all this had to be backed up with regular demonstrations of our commitment to Saudi, or Jordan, or wherever. How do you demonstrate commitment? Words are cheap; and so cash tends to do the job better.

Now some would call this corruption: the Serious Fraud Office, for one. But this was unfair. When I went to Riyadh and arranged a series of payments to senior officials, middlemen and members of the Saudi Royal Family, this wasn't corruption. We were respecting the traditions of our host country. BAe didn't want to pay this money. We'd much rather have taken it in executive bonuses or directors' share options instead. It was merely an essential business expense.

It was also our patriotic duty. How on earth could we have sold a plane like the Tornado to the Saudis, if it was up against the Mirage and the F16? Of course we had to sweeten the deal.

Also, corruption means changing people: making them corrupt. But these were merely the customs of the lands in which we were doing business. No-one was becoming *more* corrupt from the way we were doing business, so clearly no crime had been committed. Fortunately, when the SFO did finally bring charges against BAe, Tony Blair saw things clearly and blocked the prosecution on the grounds of national interest. It helped that the Saudis had threatened to kick out BAe's 4,000 employees in Saudi Arabia and cancel the whole Al Yamanah deal, which was worth something like £100 billion.

In my book, that's real sovereignty. Two sovereign nations exchanging frank views, followed by one sovereign nation (Britain) giving in to threats from another sovereign nation (Saudi Arabia). I would obviously prefer that it was Britain threatening people and throwing its weight around, like in the good old days; but that's just more incentive to Make Britain Great Again.

And one way to make money and restore Britain's international influence at the same time is to revisit David Stirling's legacy. As well as trailblazing the arms trade, he set up a marvellous outfit called Watchguard International that provided security services for a range of world leaders. From Botswana to Bahrain, any world leader with legitimacy issues or at risk of being ousted in a coup could rely on Stirling's ex-SAS colleagues to provide the best in close protection. This could range from the entry-level few chaps with guns and a plane on standby at the local airport right up to the full Monty of close support, rent-an-air-force, officers embedded in potentially disaffected military units and a counter-insurgency capability.

What this shows us is how, with a bit of can-do-ism, Britain can open up new world markets. And this neatly counters the criticism of Brexit – why, if we've failed to win export markets for the last fifty years, is it going to be different from now on? In fact, there are literally hundreds of Great British Products just waiting for the chance to have Dickie David and Blow-dry Boris help them get out and sell.

Exports

The biggest economic claim for Brexit is that we'll be free to negotiate advantageous trade deals and so boost our exports. As it happens, the British civil service doesn't have any trade negotiators: since 1973, all that's been done by the European Commission. But that just means more creative thinking, uncluttered with too much expertise. Already my own team at Brexit Solutions has identified some exciting new Priority Markets. Here's a flavour:

Burundi
Apparently, Burundi is the country in the world most likely to be placed in the wrong continent. And its very obscurity is an opportunity, for if we British have trouble finding it, where does that leave a geographically-challenged nation like America? So let's get some quintessential British products in there before the Yanks arrive: instead of Coke, we'll get them thirsting for dandelion and burdock. No Big Mac and Fries? How about a nice M+S ham sandwich with complementary Grab Bag of salt and vinegar crisps? And I expect Burundi is fairly dusty and could take a few Dysons as well.

Khazakstan
Here's a country with a lot of oil that has yet to buy some sub-standard planes from BAe and are

way down the league table of whisky exports. Some see it as a blood-stained dictatorship – I see it as an opportunity!

Desolation Island
If ever a country needed a brand make-over, it's this rocky Southern Ocean outpost. There's lots of possibilities for those creative latte-sippers to generate some astronomical fees: how about Decoration Island, Fantasy Island, or South Barbados? Or just sell off the name to the highest bidder for a bit of immortality?

It's not just new markets. We also have a slew of brilliant new products ready to go.

Jam
My very able intern Funty has discovered that less than 10% of the world's population eats jam. Well, there's an opening for our dynamic, thrusting jam industry. First, a big push on cream teas, with celebrity endorsements, recipes, competitions, Mary Berry, and, of course, 80's rock combo The Jam. The campaign will be called Jam Britannia, so that as the world turns to jam, they will also turn to British jam. Of course, the fruit will come from Europe and the sugar from the Caribbean, and even the jars will be made by a French firm (the same people we sold Pilkington's to a while back) so we'll have to flog an awful lot of jam to make up for, say, the closure of the Vauxhall factory at Ellesmere

Port. It will take time. But my motto is, jam tomorrow!

The Shower Karaoke

Two things we Brits love are singing along to our favourite popular tunes and taking showers. Put the two together and you have the Shower Karaoke, designed right here in Britain, by a British person. You hang it in the shower, take the waterproof microphone, put on Johnny Mathis or whatever, and get singing! There are add-ons such as a microphone that doubles as a back-scrubber and one for romantic shower duets. And in the SK labs they're working on an 11-man version for use in communal showers, so the England soccer team can belt out those world cup anthems after beating the Faroes or the Vatican City. Three lions on your boxers!

Mould

Apparently there are some amazing technologies out there, from intelligent carbon to nano-cars, smart wee and the internet of junk. These are the future. Britain may have missed out on one or two through a lack of investment and a tendency for our boffins to discover things and then let someone else make the money, but all is not lost. The UK are the acknowledged leaders in the cutting edge world of mould. This humble nuisance has an amazing range of properties. It can turn foodstuffs into mould. It can coat itself onto surfaces such as bath tiles and be virtually impossible to remove. Think of the possibilities. Coloured moulds that grow onto the surface as a replacement for paint. No drips, no mess, no need for a brush! Or active moulds that replace dyes on fabrics, changing shape and colour over time so your clothes never go out of fashion! 3D mould that will grow into specific shapes. Intelligent mould for storing data, that continues to grow so your computer memory never gets filled up. The possibilities are literally growing before our eyes!

Dogs
Remember when people just bought coats? Then came Burberry, Mulberry and the rest and turned the humble mac into a British Design Icon with an astonishing price tag attached. Well, it's time to do the same with dogs. After all, Britain invented dogs, and it's time we got our act together and began to push some of the foreign invaders off our turf. So we'll slap tariffs on Alsatians, Chihuahuas, Shi Tzus and the rest, and a generous subsidy regimes for honest to God British breeds such as Old English Sheepdogs, Staffordshire Terriers and, of course, the British Bulldog. And we'll be moving them up the value chain as well: King Charles Spaniels are, in effect, by Royal Appointment and should command a hefty premium. And on the day when we finally leave the EU and the fences and customs posts go up, there'll be a special commemorative issue of Border Collies. Woof woof!

Pounds

One of the reasons for championing exports post-Brexit is the need to pay for essentials from abroad, such as wines from Bordeaux and erotica from Japan. With exporting, we make things, swop them for funny money like dollars and yen, and then use those dollars and yen to buy the things we want. Well, how much easier to simply sell these foreigners pounds. We did it before with stamps. Once these were just gummy bits of paper with the Queen's head on. Then we worked out that if we kept producing 'commemorative issues' with all sorts of silly pictures on, we could sell loads and loads of extra stamps, and the great thing is, *no-one ever uses them!* Other countries are now in on the act, but there's an even bigger opportunity out there: commemorative issue pounds. Rather than changing our fivers and tenners every few years, we should have new ones coming out all the time. A set of sporting heroes one week, and British racing cars of the 1930s the next. All round the world, collectors will be snapping them up, and we'll bank the proceeds. And why stop there? Sponsored bank-notes, emblazoned with the corporate logo of Etihad or American Airlines? Why not? Britain should be in there first. After all, there's money to be made!

Hovercraft

After the war, when people began to think Britain's days as the world's inventor were over, we came up with another brilliant discovery: the hovercraft. A machine that can travel over land and water (sideways, in a stiff breeze) and make more noise than a helicopter. Britain was the first country in the world to operate the hovercraft, ferrying passengers and their cars between Dover and Calais. We were also the last one to do so. And, in fact, the only one to do so, as one of their innovative features is that they make their passengers sea-sick without touching the waves. But no matter. With the full might of the Department of International Trade behind it, the hovercraft is due a real lift-off.

So there you have it. A peek behind the curtain of the world-beating products lined up by UK Plc, just waiting to be unleashed by the creation of new tariff barriers with our largest trading partner. I'm convinced we're going to beat our international competitors hands down. Why? Wasn't it A.E. Housman who coined the tag about England using the Gatliing gun to keep down recalcitrant natives? I think those fine old words can be repurposed for Britain's Glittering Economic Miracle in the twenty-first centruy:

> *We will win, for we have got*
> *The shower karaoke, and they have not.*

PART FOUR:

FORGING A NEW BRITAIN

Sovereignty Plus

As a nation, we have voted overwhelmingly to assert our sovereignty by leaving the European Union. That's a good start. But if we're convinced we can make more money on our own, rather than as part of these international institutions, why stop there? When you start to look into it, or have your researchers look into it, you realise just how many of these international bodies there are. And there are lots of ways we're better off on our own.

Saving Cash

First, all those bodies where we pay in more than we get out. The United Nations, for example. We're not likely to need peacekeepers here any time soon, so why are we paying in to the UN club? It's the same with the World Health Organisation, UNESCO, the Food and Agriculture Organisation and literally hundreds more. Our subscriptions soon add up. And what do we get in return? No cash, that's for sure. And when was the last time we had bags of emergency flour or tents landed in the UK? So alongside leaving the EU, there's a whole alphabet soup we won't be staying with: OECD, ICOA, ICAA, IUCN, IGY, CITES, ETC, etc.

Self-regulation
Then there are all those bodies that set international rules. Why do we want any part of that? The International Maritime Organisation, for example. Do we really need a lot of foreigners to tell us how to sail our merchant ships around the world, if we had any British-registered ships left? What's even more ridiculous, in bodies like the IMO, everyone has an equal vote. Yes, not just the French, but anyone: Sudan, South Korea, Argentina, all thinking they know as much as us. That's hardly democratic is it?

Sovereignty
For years, our political elite have swanned around the world singing treaties, and these all impinge on our national sovereignty. Well, it's time to tear a few of them up and walk away. Take NATO. Apparently, if any one NATO country is invaded, then we, Britain, are duty-bound to come to their aid. This is how wars start. Think of Belgium in World War One, and Poland in World War Two. And when you start looking at who's in NATO, frankly, it's frightening. Latvia? That's almost part of Russia already, and we certainly don't want to have a war with them. Turkey? They're at daggers drawn with Iraq, Russia, Greece – the list goes on. Do we want to go to war to save Turkey? (There's a joke about Christmas in here somewhere.)

Worst of all, America is a member. Of course, they

are our oldest ally, special relationship, Pilgrim Fathers, etc etc. But think it through. We might want to go to their aid. But we might not. Much as I love Don Trump, he's not the most predictable of US Presidents, is he? You wouldn't want to bet your life savings – or more particularly, your life – on his foreign policy. War with North Korea? China? Canada? Best to sit those out, I feel. But as members of NATO, we can't.

Look at what we put in, and what we get out. We spend 2% of our national income on defence, and no-one else in NATO does that (except, the US. And Greece. Oh, and Latvia). That's £34 billion a year. And what do we get back? Nothing! Not one penny piece. (You could say that we're more secure, but that's like saying we were more secure in the European Union, because we had peace in Western Europe for sixty years. Prove it, I say!) Pull out of NATO, and we'd have £34 billion a year in our pockets. That's £654 million a week we could be spending on the NHS! Think about it!

51st State
This said, there is one institution we might want to join post-Brexit: the United States of America. Everything in the US is on a bigger scale than Europe: the meals, the cars, and the national debt (which they have to measure in trillions instead of billions). And in Don Trump they have a President to match – and a man who wants to poke the EU in the eye by offering us Brits a free trade deal. Looking good, Houston!

I know from my time at British Leyland that the US is not an easy place to do business. Some impressive British names – Tesco and M+S come quickly to mind

– have lost big trying to break into that market. And Don, though I love him dearly, is a hard bastard. I'm sure we'll get a trade deal – but we'll get screwed 'til our eyes water. After all, there's nothing an American likes better than to get one over on the Limeys. Think of the way they betrayed us over atomic power after the war. Or how much fun they had going after BP after the little matter of the *Deepwater Horizon*.

So a free trade deal is one thing – but maybe we need to think a bit bigger than that. The EU includes French Guiana, which is on the coast of South America. Why shouldn't the US extend to the other side of the Atlantic? Why shouldn't the UK become the fifty-first state to accede to the Union (and this time, the right Union?). Then we wouldn't have to worry about being royally screwed by the Americans, because we'd all *be* Americans. They might even stop having all the villains in Hollywood movies played by Brits. They could use Belgians instead.

What's in it for the Yanks, you might ask? Calvin has pointed out that, although Britain has gone a bit multicultural in recent years, it's nothing like the US. There, the whites are on course to become a minority by 2044. Another 50 million British whites would turn that around.

And once in, our natural instincts for command would help us take control and shape the US the way we wanted from inside.

Just like we did in the EU.

A Leaner, Hungrier Britain

We've seen that the British economy has a few weaknesses in there with all its strengths and opportunities, and I'd be the first to say that life after the European Union won't all be cakes and ale. For you, anyway.

But actually, a plunge in living standards will be good for Britain. We've become too soft, too flabby, too self-indulgent with all the liberal hang-ups like equality, fairness and the rule of law. We need a bit of the buccaneering, can-do, sod-the-rules spirit to return. And a bit of reality about what people can expect from life. Brexit will deliver that.

In short, we won't be able to continue as before. We'll have to tighten our belts. Throw a few inessential items overboard. Make some sacrifices.

It will be like the Great Banking Crash of 2008. Then, we needed to find gazillions of pounds to prop up our financial system. That in turn meant cutting back on luxuries like libraries, protecting the countryside and help for disabled people, and concentrating our slender resources where they would do the most good, such as incentivising people like me to make more money through tax breaks and pension top-ups. And Britain was all the better for it.

Brexit will allow us to do the same, but on a much bigger canvas. You may remember that, during the Referendum campaign, there was a lot of wild talk from the Remain camp about all the harm that would be done if we left the EU. It would hurt the NHS. It would threaten the environment. It would undermine education. And so on and so on, blah, blah, blah.

Of course, they were right. Brexit will do all those things. But is that such a bad thing? Either way, they lost, so it doesn't matter. We didn't just win Brexit in the Referendum. We won Britain. Everything that happens now can be justified by the need to make Brexit a success. That means, although Miss May might be in No 10 for the time being, it's the Brexit campaigners who hold the levers of power. They decide what Brexit looks like, and what we need to do to make it work. If anyone disagrees, they can be labelled as arrogant for failing to listen to the British people, and unpatriotic for failing to get behind Britain as we embark on this national adventure.

We have, in effect, taken over the country. We can do with it what we like. And where better to start than with education.

Education

Brexit is a wonderful chance to reshape our education system. We can streamline the curriculum, and concentrate on useful subjects such as maths, literacy, and science. Out goes anything trendy or progressive, such as media studies, psychology, art, music and religious education. Out too go all those pointless European languages that we couldn't speak anyway. (If we want English to be the world's language, why should we muck about supporting our competitors?) Grammar schools will also teach Latin and Greek, while the other schools can turn out the plumbers, electricians, bricklayers and plasterers we'll need in such huge numbers once all the Europeans have been kicked out.

But that's all pretty standard. The big changes will come in higher education. The idea that lots of our young people should go to university has been an absolute disaster. There are far too many British graduates, who should instead be apprentices or something. They also take up university places that we could be selling to foreigners.

So in the post-Brexit future we will have three tiers of universities. The first will be Oxford and Cambridge, to raise the next generation of Britain's elite. The second will be the decent, redbrick-style universities of the Russell Group, especially those strong in science like Imperial and the LSE, who we need; and these will have quotas of the better class of foreign students, paying top whack. The rest – the Kingstons, the Bradfords and so on – can become 'international universities', bringing the vast majority of their students in from overseas. That way we can keep the vital foreign exchange that universities contribute to UK Plc.

Wait a minute Reg, you will say. *Won't this create problems with all those who voted for Brexit so we could control our own borders? Won't lots of these so-called students come here on dodgy visas and then try and stay here illegally?*

Of course they would if we let them. But once again, KCK has been doing some great thinking on this. He makes the excellent point that, so long as the students stay on campus, there's no chance of them absconding. The ideal would be a university on an isolated site, surrounded by barbed wire, and with an international-standard runway attached. And lo and behold, that's exactly what we have. We simply move the current universities out of their valuable, city-centre sites and onto some of our redundant air bases. So it's Goodbye UEA and Oxford Brookes and Hello the University of Bentwaters and the Biggin Hill School of Economics. These bases have accommodation, recreation facilities, and what better way of reusing old underground bomb stores than as student bars, where they can play their jiggerty music at no inconvenience to those of us who want to retain the use of our hearing past the age of 36.

Best of all, they are very, very secure. We can fly the students in each September, fly them out again in June clutching their semi-worthless but reassuringly

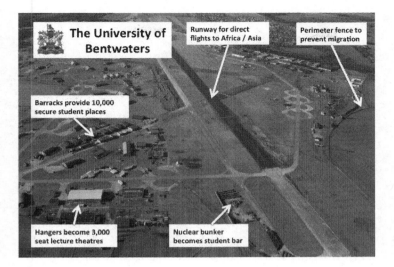

The University of Bentwaters

Runway for direct flights to Africa / Asia

Perimeter fence to prevent migration

Barracks provide 10,000 secure student places

Hangers become 3,000 seat lecture theatres

Nuclear bunker becomes student bar

expensive degrees, all at no risk of increasing the number of 'migrants' reaching the UK. Indeed, the ex-USAF bases like Bentwaters and Alconbury are technically probably not British soil at all.

KCK also points out that, just as with industry, we could have floating universities off our coasts, using old cruise ships; or simply move the universities offshore, as if they were call centres (which, let's face it, they in some ways resemble). Places like de Montford could be shipped over to India or Korea lock, stock and barrel. Best of all, those whinging, discontented, leftie, progressive university lecturers would all go too, making Britain a slightly more sane place for the rest of us.

Yes, the *Guardian* and their union friends would complain. But that, surely, us the mark of a good Brexit policy?

Health

Our much-loved National Health Service is of course at the heart of Brexit. To some – mainly the people the Leave campaign lied to so successfully – Brexit means that the NHS will gain extra resources. The sum of £350 million a week was bandied about informally. (What could be more informal that painting a number on the side of a bus?) Others thought that, if we left Europe, the NHS would suffer because it is so dependent on doctors, nurses, radiographers, lab technicians, cleaners and surgeons from the rest of the EU.

Both are wrong.

The NHS won't suffer from Brexit, or gain from Brexit, for the simple reason that it won't be there any more.

The name will stay, of course. The NHS, as a brand, has unbelievable value. But the NHS as such won't because it will be completely unaffordable. And also because of America.

To start with the money, the £350 million claim was one of KCK's most inspired moves. It was a trap for the Remainers, which they promptly waddled into. Obviously it was tosh. The only way you could come up with a figure of £350 million a week going from the UK to the EU was to add up everything we pay in and ignore everything we get back: not just cash for regional development, science, training, farming and the rest, but even the money dear Maggie won. Yes, the "£350 million" put to one side the budget rebate that Mrs T famously negotiated way back in 1981 and which has grown ever since, and is worth billions to Britain every year.

But the genius of it was that once again the dim-witted Remainers argued about how much this payment was, when they should have been banging on about the benefits of membership. Fight on the terrain of your own choosing, I was taught at Sandhurst: and how right they were. Arguing about how much we contributed simply hammered home the idea that the EU cost us money, and we could get it back.

In any case, there was never any prospect of that money – £150 million, £350 million, or any other number we might have invented – going anywhere near the NHS. When politicians have any goodies to distribute, they like to spread them around: tax cuts, defence spending, a bit on education here, on bailing out a failing business there. Add onto that the ideological hatred of the NHS amongst all right-thinking patriots, and you'll see that the NHS benefitting meaningfully from Brexit was always a pipe dream.

Hostility, my few remaining left-leaning readers will now cry? *Towards the NHS? Britain's pride and joy? Our sacred cow? Surely not.*

Which just shows how little you know about true Alt-Con thinking and the New Britain we are forging.

Remember that the NHS was created over the screaming resistance of the Conservative Party. That the Tories tried for years to introduce 'market forces' into the NHS prior to privatising it. That it was only the incredible move of the Labour Party doing this for us under Blair and Brown that allowed the NHS to be hollowed out. That most rich people wouldn't be seen dead in a NHS hospital so long as their BUPA insurance holds out.

My own views are slightly different. As a leading figure in the business community, I take the view that we are all so keen on the NHS that it's unfair to stop businesses making their own contribution: that is, by providing 'services' to the NHS such as building and managing hospitals and deciding who gets what treatment. And it has worked. More and more of the NHS is provided on a commercial basis, except that the bill still goes to the taxpayers, not the patient, while the profits go to the City – or, increasingly, to the US.

And that's where the American angle comes in. The big drive to turn the NHS into a label stuck onto private healthcare is coming from the States, where this is already the norm. What fragments of universal healthcare the US has – Medicare, for example – are paid for by the state but provided mainly by corporations. That's the model coming to the UK. Add in the right for you to take your NHS-bound tax contributions and put them into a private insurer instead, and we'll have the US system here.

And we'll have to. Once we are free of the EU and standing on our own two feet again in British Imperial splendour, we'll obviously need to do a trade deal with the US. And that in turn means offering them something. Well, quite a lot. I mean, lets be realistic about our negotiating position. Not the strongest, is it? We're leaving behind our major trading partners. We're going to woo an economy five times our size.

And we'll be up against a man who prides himself on cutting tough deals and screwing the other guy – or dame, in this case.

Ouch.

If we're lucky, we'll get a deal including free movement of people UK-US. That means a lot of those who lose their jobs here through Brexit will be able to go off to the US to find work. And there will be huge advantages in that. Britain will gain by exporting our surplus labour and getting dollar remittances – and that can soon add up to a very valuable contribution to the economy and to our balance of payments. Look at the benefit to Poland of having their people come here and send some of their earnings home, or Bangladeshi guest workers in the Gulf. And the people will gain too: sunshine, cheap petrol (sorry, gas), and no waiting around for the latest Fox box sets. Paradise.

But with free movement, the Yanks can come here too. Which is fine, I suppose. Except the main reason they'll come – more than even for the changing the guard at Buck House, to use their newly-strengthened dollars to clean out Harrods, or to buy up and asset-strip what's left of British industry – will be to freeload on the NHS. If you were wound up about health tourism under the EU, just wait until we get the US. In the rest of Europe, people were already entitled to free healthcare, so the idea of them all trundling over here was always a bit fantastical. But what you get for free in Europe would bankrupt you in the States, even if you happen to have insurance. Because one of the slight and less-publicised disadvantages of private healthcare is that, once it becomes too expensive or too long-term, the insurance switches off and you get dumped back into the publicly-funded healthcare system. Except that the US doesn't have one of those. So they'll be coming over here, discovering they have a serious condition, skipping down to the nearest GP and booking themselves in for hip replacements, heart transplants, you name it.

Except they won't, because we'll have moved the NHS onto an insurance model. No premiums, no treatment. We'll have to. Otherwise the NHS will be open to 350 million Americans to use. If you thought that the occasional Lithuanian builder in A+E who'd hit his thumb with a hammer was a crisis, just you wait. Anyone in Britain with any money will have to take out private insurance, while those who don't qualify will get some kind of emergency cover in ever-more grim public hospitals.

No, sad to say the NHS has had its day. Sad to say? Not for me personally, because I've positioned by investment portfolio to take advantage of the new opportunities in healthcare provision. But I can see that the nostalgists amongst you might regret its passing: Nye Bevan, Hattie Jacques and all that.

But as they say, you can't make a Brexit without breaking eggs!

The Environment

One of the things that sets we British apart from our European neighbours is our feelings about the natural environment. It's tremendously important to us. We get very emotional about it. And of course, when you get emotional over something, you also become inconsistent, don't you? (Ah, how that thought brings back those wonderful late-night rows with my third wife Mitzi.)

So when there were proposals for new Directives to protect birds, or habitats, or clean up rivers or cut down on air pollution, we happily signed up to them. Of course we did. We're a nation of bird-lovers. We adore the countryside. We love to go fishing. And then, when the European Commission noticed that we weren't actually implementing these new laws, they would start to complain. Crazy. You see, they didn't understand that we British also love driving everywhere, tipping toxic waste into the nearest watercourse and building on any patch of green that isn't already a golf course. And when two loves come into conflict, you have to choose the one that matters most. Which is money.

Now, as everyone knows, we British are the ones who always stick to the laws in Europe. Those ghastly Mediterranean types wouldn't recognise a law if it came at them with a flick-knife, while everyone east of Vienna merely sees the legal system as a convenient machine for generating bribes. (That Britain is actually about half-way down the list of member states for implementing European law is the kind of pseudo-fact that must clearly be wrong because it doesn't accord with what we've learned from twenty years close study of the *Daily Telegraph*.)

One reason why we are able to stick to the laws is that we have lots of lawyers, who are good at getting to the heart of what laws really mean, rather than what they say in mere words. Take air quality. The Air Quality Framework Directive says that where pollution is really bad, the government has to come up with a plan to deal with it. But as some jolly clever UK lawyers spotted, it doesn't say that plan has to be any good. So when you come across a situation in which meeting the legal limits for, say, nitrogen dioxide has the risk of inconveniencing some motorists, or preventing the expansion of a vital national resource such as Heathrow Airport, then the answer is to come up with a plan that doesn't do anything, but still has the word "Plan" written on the front. They you can stick the Plan in a jiffy bag and post it off to the Commission at 200 Rue de la Loi, Brussels 1000, Belgium, and sit back with the satisfaction of a job well done.

That's just one example of the kind of wheeze that gets Britain off the hook legal-wise, or at least lets us spin things out for a few years. I have a handy, pocket-sized guide to them kindly produced by the Cabinet Office Legal Advisers distributed to all ministers that has plenty more. Now some of you might be thinking – *this is a bit rich of us, Reg, to be lecturing Johnny Foreigner while pulling some fast ones ourselves.* But I say to you, Britain needs no lectures on this. We understand that wrapping the environment up in all kinds of protection is not going to do it any favours in the long term. The countryside needs a bit of Tough Love. Too much protection is going against Mother Nature herself.

Is not Britain the country that discovered Natural Selection and Survival of the Fittest? And who is the Commission to go against that? If a species of bird or beetle or whatever finds it cannot fit into Britain's evolving landscape, then it ought to move offshore. If it cannot make a decent return from living in a meadow or wood, then it ought to let that land go for a more productive use, such as an estate of executive-style dwellings or a retail park. In a modern, post-Brexit Britain, we certainly can't carry any passengers, and that applies to newts and skylarks as much as anyone else. Look at foxes. As their traditional habitats have been destroyed, they've got on their bikes and looked for food. Watching the russet vermin picking over the contents of my neighbour's bins, I am seeing Mother Nature in action.

After all, when humans can't find work, we don't cosset them with proper retraining or a reasonable level of unemployment benefit, do we? Of course not. We expect them to use the bracing, character-forming stimulus of homelessness and hunger to focus their energies on seeking employment. And if it's right for our fellow citizens to be encouraged to make use of natural resources such as food waste in bins and the accommodation opportunities of railway arches, should animals expect a free ride?

Under Brexit, Britain will have a truly British approach to the environment. Protection for the bits that matter.

Flexibility to promote a bit of wealth creation. And the use of prevailing winds and currents to export as much sulphur dioxide and radioactive effluent to our French, Dutch and Irish friends as we can.

National Assets

When I began my long and fruitful career, the Balance of Payments was a constant issue for Britain. For my younger readers, to whom it may now seem an economic irrelevance, some words of explanation may be helpful.

If I buy something from abroad, I will probably have to pay for it in a different currency, and that brings up the question of the exchange rate between the two countries. If I buy and sell the same amounts internationally each year, then everything is OK, because the money coming in balances with the money going out. But if I buy more than I sell, then I am going to need extra cash to pay for the imports. I might have to use pounds to buy dollars. And as demand for dollars goes up, the relative value of dollars and pounds changes. Essentially, pounds become worth a tiny bit less, and dollars a tiny but more.

And when you add up all the millions of transactions, this can start to matter. In its most extreme form, if you buy in from abroad far more than you export, measured by the 'balance of payments', then your currency begins to fall in value quite sharply. And if currency traders see this, and anticipate this continuing, then they will have all the more reason to sell their own holdings, or bet against the value of the pound remaining stable. So you have a 'run' on the currency. That makes imports more expensive, and you get inflation.

But Britain, under the sainted Maggie, found a way round this. The balance of payments are like the accounts of a business, recording what you've paid for raw materials, labour and so on and what you get for sales. If you go on making a loss each year, eventually you go bust (or if you have the right connections, you get bailed out by the Government). A business in trouble can put off the evil day by selling its capital assets (buildings, land, other companies and so on) and treating the money it receives as income. This is, however, illegal, for the very reason that it can be used to hoodwink banks, shareholders and creditors about the financial health or otherwise of the business. The disposal of capital is a one-off: unlike income, it can't be replicated the following year, except by finding other assets to sell.

But national accounts have no such restrictions. If you take an asset such as British Airways, which is wholly owned by the British government, and sell it off; and if half those share end up in the hands of overseas investors, you have in effect 'exported' half of BA, and the cash the government receives help keep the balance of payments in balance.

Throughout the privatisation programme under Labour and Tories, British assets have become part-owned – sometimes even fully-owned – by overseas investors. The result has been that we've been able to run massive deficits on the balance of payments year after year.

But this can't continue for much longer. First, as North Sea Oil dries up, the gap between our imports and exports will get bigger. But also, the one problem with selling assets abroad is that any money those assets make will leave the country in dividends, instead of going to British shareholders. So although selling assets papers over the cracks, those cracks do keep getting wider year on year.

In response, we need to think boldly.

Britain is one of the world's great brands. People love British stuff. The pageantry. The historic castles. The beautiful countryside. The stately homes. That place where they filmed *Poldark*. It all adds up to a vast reserve of cultural assets.

And in a very real sense, these are assets that belongs to the world, not just to Britain. Just as Shakespeare's words still inspire cotton workers in Bangladesh or drug dealers in Chicago's south side, so our great houses, our woodlands, our rugged coasts and glorious beaches, our moors and mountains – all these belong to the whole human race.

And making this more than a rhetorical flourish is easier than you think.

The National Trust, for example. Why should the ownership of this venerable institution be vested only in the British people, when it truly belongs to the world. And when it is transformed into NT Plc, and shares are offered on the London Stock Exchange, then the world will be able to become a real stakeholder in the Trust and its important works.

And some international figures might wish to go further. Most people who visit the properties of the National Trust want to do one of three things: walk the dog; visit the tea room; or give themselves a few minutes respite from their awful brood. None of these things is much to do with the house itself. So we could lease off the majority of these places to Russian oligarchs or Indian entrepreneurs, and both raise some much-needed foreign currency and engage in a form of cultural diplomacy with the world's movers and shakers.

It isn't just the Trust, you know. English Heritage have hundreds of castles, stately homes and ancient monuments. Some are not getting the love and attention they deserve, and might be better off in foreign hands. Stonehenge, for example: conservationists are always grumbling about how the majesty and peace of the site is spoiled by its proximity to the A303. Well, I say, if the Ancient Britons wanted their stones to be special and sacred, why did they build it right next to one of the main traffic routes to the South-West? And if UNESCO and other international do-gooders don't think we're looking after Stonehenge properly, then why don't they spend some cash on it? Meanwhile, my preference is to see Britain as at the heart of a cultural nexus, in which we shouldn't worry too much about who owns what or where it is based. We have the Elgin Marbles. China gets Stonehenge. What's the problem?

When the Government tried to sell off Britain's forest a few years back, there was a bit of an outcry from some fringe elements such as 500,000 middle class dog-walkers and the Archbishop of Canterbury. A shame: but, typically, Cameron did not make the case properly. When Nigel comes to sell off the Forestry Commission, things will be very different. First, the economy will be comprehensively (if temporarily) screwed up by the minor, passing transitional impact of Brexit. But more than that, we can explain that we want people to be closer to their natural environment, whether that is people like you staying in those odd little log chalets, or people like me buying up 50,000 acres, closing it off to the public and building a fuck-off mansion with helipad, separate underground servants' quarters and discrete anti-insurrection measures, in the middle of it.

After all, it's all about being close to Mother Nature, isn't it?

The Challenge

So, we've seen that Brexit – while a wonderful opportunity for Britain – does present some challenges. Now is a good time to summarise and reflect on the three most challenging challenges:

"How to make money from foreigners without having too much to do with them."

"How to turn back the clock to 1953 without anyone noticing."

"How to destroy the European Union."

How to make money from foreigners without having too much to do with them

Britain has been an international trading nation for centuries. We've made an awful lot of money from this down the years – trading in cotton, sugar and slaves; creating colonies to exploit the wealth of new lands; developing natural resources like copper, tin and bauxite; building ports, railways and other profitable infrastructure; and above all, selling stuff to foreigners – from tanks to talcum powder, slaves to Sunbeam Alpines, opium to... (Hang on! That's an idea. Didn't we used to have a big opium export thing going in China? Might be time to get that back on its feet.)

Anyway, that was fine when the foreigners stayed

foreign. But increasingly, as the world becomes inter-connected, international trade means foreigners coming to Britain. And not just staying in the East End of London weaving cloth like the Huguenots, but getting everywhere – in our universities, in our board-rooms, on TV, and even in our gambling clubs.

In a way, the lumpen, ignorant, prejudiced, pizza-and curry-guzzling masses were ahead of us in seeing that this was not good for Britain. But now we are alive to the danger, we must act decisively. Hence the challenge to maintain trade, make money, but not let the buggers in – unless they have an awful lot of ready cash.

Selling citizenship is the obvious first step. A million pounds for a British passport seems like a good starting-point.

Then there's setting conditions for the foreigners who do come – like the Homelands idea, the university camps, and the off-shore industrial estates.

And we could make some space with some emigration of our own. As we deepen our relations with the Old Empire – Canada, Australia, the United States and so on – there will surely be opportunities to export some of our surplus population. There are still plenty of places in the world – not just Spain – where British people are happy to settle down and feel superior to those around them.

As always, Don Trump is ahead of the game on this. We simply make things very unpleasant for any foreigner, unless they have a lot of money. If anyone complains, that's good – it shows to your power-base that you're doing the right thing. And as always with splitting the country down the middle, the trick is to claim to be patriotic and make sure you have the half with the guns on your side.

How to turn back the clock to 1953 without anyone noticing

This is the big prize. Yes, we can get rid of all that Euro-legislation by playing fast and loose with the Great Repeal Act and going on about having to pay our way in the world. But what we really need to do is take the once in a generation opportunity to really get rid of the progressive ideas of the 1960s.

Think back to 1953. Edmund Hilary planting a Union Jack at the top of Everest as the Queen's coronation heralded a New Elizabethan Age. Windscale offering electricity too cheap to bother metering. The Comet ready to beat the world. The sun still not setting on an Empire in which the Royal Navy sailed proudly from Hong Kong to Aden and white farmers were still exploiting the potential of Rhodesia, the Gold Coast and Kenya. Winston Churchill was in No 10 and *The Cruel Sea* on at the local Odeon. The horrors of meritocracy, satire, feminism and Jacques Delors were all still in the future. It was, perhaps, Britain's Finest Hour.

But these days can come again. Deregulation will allow us to sweep away all the petty-fogging nit-picking rules about discrimination. If we cut business taxes enough, there won't be much money left for local government, and they'll sack all their equality and diversity officers. Get our young people out of the universities and back to work, and scrap all those employment protections at the same time, the industrial tribunals and so on, and we'll get a bit more deference back into the system.

And once people are back in their place, they'll be happier. This idea of the working classes bettering themselves was always a mistake. Yes, a few clever grammar school boys making good, if you really insist. The odd barmaid marrying into the aristocracy to enhance the gene pool does no harm. But most of the time, we all just want to know where we are in the hierarchy: people like me at the top, people like you quite a bit further down. You're happy to look up to me, because the system makes sure there's always someone you can look down on. Poor people. Keith Chegwin. It doesn't matter who, so long as you're not at the bottom yourself.

How to destroy the European Union

Thinking ahead to 2019, the biggest threat to the Futtock Vision is the continued existence of the European Project. What if it is a success? What if it continues to deliver peace and prosperity while Britain starts to resemble some of the less attractive parts of Detroit? What if – God forbid – people start wondering if they made the right choice to leave?

Also, the EU is a powerful trading block. How much easier life would be if we could strike deals with individual member states.

Like the first moment you think of murdering your wife, this idea has an air of unreality. You wouldn't really do it, would you? But you might enjoy thinking about it, even planning it. And then, somehow, it's easier to cross the boundary from dream to reality.

Well, I'm ahead of you on that path, having had some prior experience. (Though this has nothing to do with by fourth wife Rose-Mae's untimely end – she simply didn't see the combine harvester coming.) We've already set up a Task Force within the BS Secretariat to plan ways of sowing division in Europe – for example, channelling money to anti-European political parties; funding bogus research through faked-up research institutes that the BBC treats as real; running supposed 'grassroots' campaigns to discredit the EU institutions; and generating fake news about MEP expenses, corruption, and the rest.

We know this will work because it's what the Alt Right in the US did in Britain before the EU referendum, with a bit of top-up help from some fascists and Vlad Putin. Psychological warfare, black ops, and the rest were pretty much invented by the British (before being refined by the Yanks in Vietnam and updated for the internet age by the tobacco and oil majors).

And if it doesn't work, then maybe some low-key backing for separatist movements: after all, Britain has always supported those fighting for freedom. I'm thinking a few arms shipments, some training in sabotage. As Churchill memorably said, "Set Europe Ablaze!"

The Negotiations

Now these challenges may make it seem as if there's a lot riding on the negotiations.

In which case, I'm sorry to say you haven't been paying attention.

First, if the negotiations mattered, do you think David Davis would be put in charge of them?

Second, if we're supposed to be leaving Europe because of forty years of failing to negotiate a good deal from the slimy so-and-sos, then why do you think that on this occasion – as we pass through the door marked *Adios* – that we'll do any better?

But most of all, because there aren't going to be any negotiations.

Oh sure, we'll keep going off there and sit in a room, with officials scurrying round clasping files of papers. We'll make various statements. We'll appear at odd hours of the day and night for the cameras looking tight-lipped. All that guff.

But we're not actually trying to negotiate anything. After all, there isn't a deal to be done, is there?

Say you're a member of a golf club, and one of the other members announces that they're leaving, they won't be paying their subs any more, and might even join another club – but they'd still like to keep playing on your course whenever they felt like it, and maybe drop in to the bar after for a snifter. Except they also won't stick to your rules when they do so, and if they want to use the Secretary's reserved space in the car park, so be it. If they did, you'd tell them where to get off, wouldn't you? You certainly wouldn't offer them a "deal".

But that suits us fine. Fifty-one percent of the British people voted for Brexit. We don't need to win over the other 49% to keep the "democratic will" tosh that is the basis of our English coup. And how do we do that? By proving that the Europeans were a bunch of shits, just like we always said they were. At every turn in the "negotiations," the trick is to allow the media to portray it as Evil Brussels – populated solely by stage demons like Juncker and Schutlz – plotting to Do Britain Down.

It's going to work, too. After all, we're talking about convincing a bunch of people who thought that a City stockbroker called Nigel wanted to improve the lives of people in Spalding or Burnley or wherever, while also finding extra money for the NHS.

And human nature will help. All those who kindly voted for us to leave now face a psychological dilemma. As the shit is liberally sprayed the length and breadth of Britain – the pound worth less and less, all the well-paid City jobs leeching away to Paris and Dublin, and Spanish tomatoes, Dutch eggs and Danish bacon shooting up in price so that even a Great British Breakfast has a 20% Brexit surcharge on it – do these people say "Oh no, I really mucked that up with that vote. If only I'd listened to David Cameron. Instead I've condemned the country I love to an economic and social catastrophe the like of which I haven't seen since Harold Wilson was Prime Minister." Or do they say "Yes! I knew it! Those ungrateful bastards won't even give us unfettered access to the Single Market. We're better off out."

That's what the 51% want – nay, need – to see. And we're going to give it to them. When Little Miss May said 'No deal is better than a bad deal', she was half-right. In fact, no deal is better than any deal, for how can any deal satisfy politicians like Farage or Mogg who have built their whole career on being against Europe. It's like those fools who, during the French Revolution, thought it might be wise to keep the monarchy in some form. They were outflanked by the Ultras, and before they knew it were on their way to the guillotine. Well, that's not where Reg Futtock plans to end up, I can tell you!

So we want the negotiaitons to fail. That's simple enough. We've started by claiming, against all the evidence, that it's clearly in the interest of the European Union to give Britain a deal in which we maintain full and unrestricted access to the Single Market without being subject to any of the irksome rules, or making any kind of financial contribution.

That makes it eminently sensible to have what I've christened Futtocks Five Red Lines:

1. We don't pay in anything at all. But we'll help ourselves to anything going.

2. British people can live in Europe, but Europeans can't come here unless they already own a house here, have BUPA insurance and can sing the third verse of *Rule, Britannia!* (including the tricky pizzicato bit).

3. Our 'workers' (lawyers, bankers, tax evasion advisors, etc) are free to live and work anywhere in Europe; but their 'workers' (plumbers, electricians, nurses, etc) are not. Unless we want them after all.

4. We absolutely refuse to have anything at all with the European Court of Justice. We'd rather the ECJ just decided any legal cases about British trade in the Single Market themselves, rather than the UK being able to make representations, appoint judges to the Court, etc etc.

5. We will die on the barricades to protect the plucky, hearts of oak residents of Gibraltar from the olive-oil drenched hands of the Spanish, even though we completely forgot about them until the EU reminded us.

To manage the negotiations up to the point of irretrievable collapse, and because he's not the sharpest knive in the drawer, I've given Dickie some pretty clear advice about Futtock's Three Stages of Brexit Negotiations.

Good Faith
In the first stage, we'll come up with a series of Position Papers which give the impression that we are engaging with the negotiations in good faith, but which do not contain any actual positions. Why? Because positions require some engagement with reality, and let me assure you that the last thing we British need at this stage

is even a whiff of that. Instead, these papers will rigorously focus on how we want to let everything we like (London as the financial hub of Europe, cheap flights to Bordeaux) to stay the same, and not spending too much time on less helpful details like how we want to kick out millions of EU citizensand not pay our bills. The key is to make us look very, very reasonable.

Betrayal
In the second phase, we move on to express our shock that the EU is trying to Do Britain Down. We have expressed some wonderful sentiments in our Position Papers – about how we will work together to ensure prosperity, security, frictionless borders etc – and now the EU are trying to stiff us with typically pettifogging, bureaucratic questions such as 'What do you actually want?' In this stage, the blame for the fact that nothing promised to the British people during the referendum is remotely deliverable can be quietly shifted to the Europeans.

The Military Option
The Betrayal stage will keep the 51% happy. But remember, we'll have a leadership contest going on in the background, with Johnson, Gove, Moggie and the rest briefing against each other in all the papers. How, then, to we Bring Britain (for which read the Conservative Party) Together? Jingoism, of course. We choose a cause – in a way, the more bogus and irrelevant,

Strategic Project Delivery Alignment Gateway Review

Presentation by the BS Team

Our Three Priorities

* How to make money from foreigners while maintaining Britain's utter isolation

* How to turn back the clock to 1953

* How to destroy the European Union

Negotiation Milestones

Good Faith › Betrayal › Military Options › No Deal

Current Status

- We have made excellent progress since the previous milestone:
  - We have succeeded in not making any proposals
  - We have not clarified any of our positions
  - We have painted the EU as greedy and inflexible
- Now we are ready to:
  - Blame the EU for refusing to discuss our future trading relationships
  - Refuse to make any financial settlement
  - Raise fears of war breaking out over Ireland / Gibraltar / Flanders / Calais

Escalating the Rhetoric Delivery

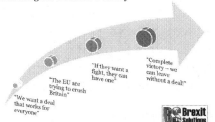

"We want a deal that works for everyone"

"The EU are trying to crush Britain"

"If they want a fight, they can have one"

"Complete victory – we can leave without a deal!"

Operation Blame Game

- Critical to blame EU for economic and social consequences of Brexit
- Establish British good faith through constant repetition of key terms:
  - flexible approach
  - imaginative solutions
  - everyone's best interests
  - still part of Europe
- Absolute ban on UK taking any positions whatsoever, particularly on money

the better, because then people understand it less and won't ask any awkward questions – and start drawing some red lines in the sand.

The obvious cause for a bit of sabre-rattling is Gibraltar. A hard border with Spain would be a disaster for Gibraltar. But Spanish pride is not going to put up with a deal where they get nothing. So we make a stand on this, ratchet up the rhetoric, and wait for our more flammable MPs (Bone, perhaps? Chope?) to start referring nostalgically to the Falklands as the last time we showed some Hispanic types where they got off.

As things heat up, we can tip a consignment of their tomatoes into the sea at Portsmouth. They'll retaliate by closing the border with Gibraltar. We seize some of their fishing vessels off Cornwall. Before you know it, the Defence Secretary will be refusing to confirm or deny that our Trident missiles are trained on Alicante or Barcelona, Johnson will become even more ridiculously Churchillian, and anyone who disagrees with the hardest possible Brexit will be a Spanish-loving sell-out merchant ready to be demonised in every newspaper and perhaps even symbolically flung from a church tower.

Gotcha!

In fact, Gibraltar may not be the best *causus bellus fabricatus*. Yes, we had a dry run in the spring of 2017 that went pretty well. But 97% of Gibraltarians voted to remain in the EU, which isn't the strongest foundation for a really good international incident. (Imagine if 97% of Falkland Islanders had wanted to become part of Argentina? Where would Maggie be now?)

No, the front-runner is the Commonwealth War Graves Commission. It ticks all the boxes. Obscure? Yes. Potentially highly emotive? Check. Likely to wrong-foot the Europeans? Check.

It goes like this. There are over a million British soldiers buried in cemeteries on the continent, mainly in Belgium and northern France, who died for our country. If we're going to use people currently alive as bargaining chips in this negotiation, then surely it makes sense to use the dead too. So we're planning a tabloid campaign to stir up the blood of all true Englishmen and women. Currently, descendants of the fallen can travel to the battlefields of Flanders with just their passport. Once we've left, they may need a visa. Implicit in the idea of a visa is that the country you are visiting – France, Belgium, and so on – might refuse. So we have the spectre of grieving relatives being denied access to their loved ones by the heartless actions of a bunch of continental surrender-monkeys. We're working on some suitable headlines, such as **EU HOLDS DEAD BRITISH SOLDIERS FOR RANSOM.**

With a bit of luck, we'll provoke an obscure German MEP into saying something regrettable, and we'll be able to drag in the Nazis, and soon all patriotic Britons will be joining the Local Defence Volunteers and burning down pubs selling German lager.

The more of these bogus stories, the better. We've got a whole team of former hacks working in the Brexit Solutions secretariat on these, including:

- Revelations of an EU plan to release rabies into Britain unless we agree to hand back the Channel Islands.

- Threats by the French to turn off the electricity inter-connector to Britain during *Eastenders / Great British Bake-off* Final.

- Plans by the European Commission to hold a leaving party for Britain on 27 March 2019 at Dunkirk, complete with a giant 'Sorry You're Leaving' card signed by the remaining 27 member states and a £20 M+S voucher, purchased after a whip-round of all 350 million Europeans.

- The creation of a new EU radio station to broadcast propaganda into Britain. Provisionally named Radio Free Angleterre, it will be staffed by Anglo-Quislings such as Danny Boyle and Gary Linaker.

Can't you just imagine the great soccer luvvie (what has he ever done for England, I ask myself) presenting *Le Match du Jour* on TF1, with highlights of football matches in which there are no English players, and then bemoaning the state of English football with other effete sell-out merchants such as Rio Ferdinand and David Beckham. Even the BBC wouldn't stoop that low!

High-Friction Borders

But the best point of conflict will, as always, be Ireland. Clearly there will have to be a border between the Republic of Ireland, still part of the EU, and the United Kingdom of Great Britain and Northern Ireland. If we have a land border running between Ulster and the Republic, that will set back the Peace Process a decade. And if we have a sea border between Ulster and the Mainland, then it will send the Peace Process back to 1689. But in the Good Faith stage, we can avoid being seen to take a position on this by talking about "imaginative solutions" and "frictionless borders".

In the second stage, we can round on the Commission, who will have somehow failed to come up with any imaginative solutions to awkward questions such as "where do you want the customs posts to be?"

And in the third stage, our good friends in the Most Loyal Order of Orange Rebels Who Refuse To Be Told By Her Majesty The Queen Or Any Other Traitors To Have Anything To Do With The Fucking Papists will begin to buy lots of guns, march up and down in orange berets and generally say No a lot. Negotiations with the EU will break down. We'll have a hard border with the South, consisting of customs posts, watchtowers, razor-wire, minefields, and 2 Para – just like the old days. After that, having a friction-heavy border at

Dover or Harwich won't look too bad.

So that's the negotiations in a nutshell. We don't just ensure they fail. We ensure they fail *on our terms*. And then The Plan can go fully into operation.

The Plan

By this time, you're probably wondering why the number of pages left of this book keeps going down, but we haven't yet got to The Plan.

You may also be wondering how it is that all the supposed ways in which Britain will prosper in the future seem to be duds. British manufacturing, you have seen, will never recapture its lost world markets, and we're so far behind in most aspects of technology that this isn't going to make up the difference. The service sector will take a huge hit under Brexit. Retail won't work in overseas markets, and defence and security is already dragging in as much cash for the country as we could realistically expect, so there's no hope there. Property and the sales of assets will keep UK Plc afloat for a while through some creative accounting, but ordinary people won't have a look-in on that. And finance is really for the wealthy to become more wealthy, and anyway none of those people will be paying any tax in thrusting, dynamic, wealth-creation-friendly Brexit Britain. Only deregulation offers any real prospect of making Britain more competitive internationally, and the slight problem with that is that the one thing it won't do is improve your quality of life. Quite the opposite, as you'll find out when your pension disappears, your taps start emitting methane gas and your children succumb to asbestosis.

So you want a Plan; and you want to know that

you, and those close to you, will be All Right.

This is the chapter that answers your concerns. It sets out The Plan, and explains why this is the right – indeed, the only – way forward for Britain.

To start with a brief recap.

We've seen that Britain joined the European Union for the right reasons, even if we mucked about in our usual way and joined twenty years later than we could or should have done.

We've seen that Britain did well economically during our time in the European Union. After a long period of comparative economic decline after 1945, we stabilised things, and began to turn them around. The EU helped. So too did discovering squillions of pounds worth of oil and gas in the North Sea. True, our manufacturing never recovered its old dominance, and a lot of it was assembling things for US and Japanese companies; but we did well in financial and professional services, so it just about evened out.

People in Britain were relaxed about being in the EU. Not very enthusiastic, but not troubled either. This was because the 'ever-closer Union' didn't affect people's everyday lives. You could still drink pints and the road signs were still in miles.

But there were still business people who wanted to have an Atlantic or even Empire outlook. They joined forces with the cranks and weirdoes who are now my good friends in UKIP to run a twenty-year campaign to discredit the EU and persuade the British people to vote to leave. The main success was in having lots of anti-EU candidates selected by the ghastly types who infest the local Conservative parties, and who in turn created so much trouble for successive Tory leaders that they were promised a Referendum to get them to shut up. Once the EU was connected to people's perfectly understandable racist concerns about immigration, the referendum was lost.

And so we look to the future. Britain is leaving, but on what terms?

We've seen that there is no good deal to be had. No favours, no special treatment. We can trade with the EU, but we'll be outsiders. The rules of the Single Market will not work in our favour, and may be used to screw us. The City of London will gently shift towards Paris and Frankfurt. Our trade deficit with the rest of Europe will deepen. Sterling will continue to lose value internationally, which will help our exports, but also leave us worse off (or rather, leave you lot worse off: my money will be banked offshore in Swiss francs and euros.)

In Britain, we'll lose a huge amount of investment from overseas, and we'll struggle to replace the hundreds of thousands of skilled Europeans who will head off elsewhere. We'll have fewer French doctors and Spanish nurses in the NHS, and have to ransack the health services of the third world to bring in their replacements. If there really were a dividend of £350 million a week for the NHS from leaving the EU, it would be swallowed up in paying the extra wages and covering up the huge disruption that Brexit will bring. Unfortunately, that £350 million a week was just a lie painted on the side of a bus.

And the new trade deals we can strike with the vibrant, exciting markets of Asia? Well, trade depends on an exchange. Countries like India don't want to buy lots more stuff from us. They can make their own steel and cars (and as we've seen, they already own our steelworks and our most successful car plants). They might want our professional services, but in return they will want to export their greatest asset: their people. Without free movement of people, deals with countries like India will only ever be fiddling at the margins. And it's hard to see the British people putting up with leaving the EU because they don't like foreigners, and then welcoming the idea of allowing anyone from India or China to come here to work.

Now I can here you saying really quite loudly: *Come on Reg! The Plan! Now! What is it?*

It's simple. Very, very simple.

The Plan is, that there is no Plan.

Why? Because we don't need one.

By we, I don't mean you and the millions of other Britons who are caught up in this.

I mean, we, the people who run Britain.

Were going to be fine, thanks. In Europe, out of Europe. Deal with India, no deal with India. Sterling up, Sterling down. Exports up, down, looping the loop, it all just doesn't matter.

For at its the heart, Brexit is about control. Do we run things in Britain, the way we want? Or do we let a bunch of foreigners interfere?

Interfere with screwing down wages, building over the countryside, avoiding taxes and continuing to ensure that people like me stay on top of the pile.

Under Brexit, we get to do all of that.

Yes, the economy will be mildly fucked up. But even

if some of the businesses I am involved with suffer, I'll be looked after. Directors' emoluments, pension contributions, and all the rest of it will be ring-fenced.

And Brexit will be rather fun. No more boring collaboration. A firm hand on the tiller once more. It doesn't matter if we're heading for the rocks, the great thing is to be the Captain.

There's an irony in this somewhere, I suppose.

Maybe it's in the way that the Brexit campaign told everyone it was a vote to 'take back our country'.

You did it. You took it back for us.

We, the natural rulers of Britain, we thank you.

Now kindly fuck off back to your ghastly leather-effect sofas, your Sky packages, and your oven-ready pizzas and let us get on with it.